Harry Postlethwaite

with additional research by

John Senior and Bob Rowe

Computer Origination, Design and Layout by John A Senior

Contents

	Acknowledgements	Inside front cover
	Introduction	3
	Map of Tramcar and Omnibus routes as at 1932	6
1	The Horse Drawn Era	8
2	Towards Electric Traction	13
3	Stockport Corporation Tramways	14
4	The First Motor Buses – 1908	23
5	The Trackless Trolleybuses 1913-1920	26
6	The 'British' Buses of the BAT Company	32
7	Other Events between 1910 and the 1920s	36
8	Stockport's own first Motor Buses now arrive	40
9	Development during the Busy 1920s	42
10	Inter-urban Express Bus Services	54
11	Greater Emphasis on the Buses Now	58
12	Wartime	77
13	Post War Developments	86
14	Decision time for The Trams	101
15	Events in the 1950s	118
16	1960s: The Final Years	132
17	Going down, but going down fighting	146

Appendices

1	Tramcar Fleet List	148
2	Bus Fleet List 1913-1969	149
3	Commencement Dates for Bus Services 1913-1951	151
4	Schedule of Tram and Bus Services as at 1938	152
5	Schedule of Bus Services as at 1963	153
6	Joint Operation	154
7	Memories of Mersey Square	155
8	Tickets	160
9	Buses in Service	162
10	List of Preserved vehicles	168

Front cover illustration:

One of Stockport's Leyland-bodied Leyland Titans in the Square outside the fire station. *(RGR)*

Rear cover illustration:

Garter and Coats of Arms as carried on vehicles. *(Garter courtesy Cliff Marsh; All photography JAS)*

INTRODUCTION

The town of Stockport is situated in the County of Greater Manchester and forms the southern boundary of that county. Prior to local government reorganisation in 1974 it was situated in the County of Cheshire and was the second largest town in that county to Birkenhead. It was situated on the northern fringe of the county and the boundary of the County Borough coincided with the county boundary and also part of the boundary of the City of Manchester which was, in those days, situated in Lancashire.

It had the second largest municipal bus fleet in the county of Cheshire, the largest being at the opposite end of the county in Birkenhead. The A6 trunk road runs through the centre of the town and in earlier times this had brought transport to the fore as merchants and others travelled to Birmingham and London from Manchester and further afield. Remaining mill chimneys visible on the skyline give reminders of the town's more recent industrial past, while some of the mills remain standing, but in use for new purposes.

Without question, however, the dominating features of the town are the huge sandstone cliffs alongside the motorway (and before that the east-west railway line), containing a labyrinth of tunnels used as air raid shelters and capable of housing 5,000 souls, and towering above that same motorway as it crosses it, the 111ft high vast four-track railway viaduct linking the town with Manchester, northern England and Scotland to the north, and Crewe, Birmingham and London to the south. Opened in 1842, and using 11 million red bricks, it was at the time the largest in the world; it was later extended by the addition in 1887-9 of a parallel construction immediately alongside the original. The resultant structure is claimed to have been the first four-track brick railway viaduct in Europe, if not the world. In 1989 it was given a £3m restoration and facelift, being floodlit at the same time so that it now dominates the valley at night time as it does during the day.

The first recorded reference to Stockport, as 'Stokeport', can be traced back to 1170. But it seems clear that the Romans regarded the point where a ford crossed the River Mersey as worthy

One of a series of photographs taken from this spot, this one was apparently chosen by George Cardwell to hang in his office, reminding him, and his successors, of how the battle to gain entry into Stockport was eventually won. He would also remember that Stockport had tried to persuade him to take over the operation of the trackless Offerton route, the wiring for whose trolley buses can be seen suspended from the poles in the centre of this view. It provides a wonderful panorama with Manchester-bound trains crossing the high level viaduct, the A6 climbing away to the left towards Hazel Grove and an Edgeley-bound tram about to pass in front of the single-decker bus. British became North Western Road Car Co Ltd soon after this picture was taken. *(Courtesy Walter Womar)*

of some fortification to protect this facility, and it is remarkable that this crossing, where the A6 trunk road crosses this river, is still the centre of modern-day Stockport nearly two millennia later. It is this long established highway, for many centuries the main route from Manchester to London, which sustained the existence of Stockport. By 1834 there were some 15 stage coach owners regularly providing dependable and reliable – if perhaps uncomfortable – connections for those wishing or needing to travel to Manchester (five owners offering 40 return journeys every weekday), Birmingham and Nottingham (another five to each) whilst more locally Macclesfield, Derby and Buxton were served. Five London-bound coaches departed from Stockport each day and night with a journey time of over 18 hours.

In later times the A6 brought its own problems in regard to severe traffic congestion. The M60 orbital motorway, which runs under the railway viaduct and along the trackbed of a line which was much used for the transport of coal from Yorkshire to Lancashire Power Stations, has more-recently helped relieve much of this congestion.

Today much of the River Mersey has been built over by the Merseyway Shopping Centre – the Mersey begins in Stockport, of course, at the confluence of the Rivers Goyt and Tame. The first borough charter was granted around 1260 and for nearly 600 years was the basis for local government of the town. The existence of the charter permitted the holding of a market, and

right up to today Stockport's market is a major attraction for shoppers. In the late Victorian period a Jewish refugee from Belarus ran a market stall in Stockport, before linking up with one Thomas Spencer and opening a store in Manchester. Marks' Christian name was the impetus for his son to introduce the 'St Michael' brand name.

From the 17th century Stockport became a centre for the hatting industry and rapid expansion took place during the Industrial Revolution. At its height during the 19th century there were 100 hat factories and businesses, employing some 10,000 men, women and children. The use of silk, produced in nearby Macclesfield, was a particular speciality. As a result the town boasts the UK's only hat museum, the 'Hat Works' based in Wellington Mill, once one of the thriving Victorian hat factories and replacing the earlier museum in the former famous Battersby's 'Hat Factory' in Hempshaw Lane.

The town had been connected to the national canal network by the five miles of the Stockport branch of the Ashton Canal which was opened in 1797, but it was the arrival of railway passenger services in 1843 that had most impact, not the least of which was the visual one, the dominance of which has already been mentioned. The artist LS Lowry was much taken by the viaduct and it appeared in many of his industrial landscapes.

Municipal pride exemplified – Stockport's fire station, opened on 10th April 1902 was a fine and imposing building. *(NDC)*

The 1835 Municipal Corporations Act made Stockport a municipal borough, its status being raised to that of County Borough of Stockport in 1889, as a result of the Local Government Act passed the previous year. Generally to achieve County Borough status a town's population had to exceed 50,000. In 1901, Reddish was incorporated into the borough, having itself become an Urban District in 1894. The Stockport Branch canal passed through Reddish.

Reddish was historically part of Lancashire and developed rapidly during the Industrial Revolution and still retains landmarks from that period, such as Houldsworth Mill, a former textile manufactory. The transfer of the district into Cheshire was not universally popular, but Stockport was delighted, gaining tax income and building land, in return for which Reddish received various civic amenities, including a combined fire station, free library and baths, not forgetting of course a new tramway.

One of the most interesting buildings in the borough is the Town Hall, designed by Sir Alfred Brunwell Thomas and opened in 1908 in the Baroque Revival style and bearing more than a passing resemblance to Belfast City Hall, designed in the same style by the same architect and opened two years earlier.

Engineering was also important with names such as Crossley, Mirrlees, and Cravens – machine tools not buses and trams – being synonymous with the town's prosperity, and providing the need for reliable local transport. Perhaps the best known to bus enthusiasts worldwide would be Autovac, a company located on Wellington Road North, Heaton Norris, from 1920 and whose fuel pumps graced the external bulkhead of thousands of buses, often providing the ideal spot to apply the fleet number.

At Woodford, Avro's factory provided a vital contribution to the war effort, with many of the famous Lancaster bombers being built there and later the equally-famous range of V bombers.

A more pleasant transport link with Germany can be found with the twinning of the town with Heilbronn, an attractive town in southern Germany situated between Stuttgart and Heidelberg. In the pavement in front of the Rathous (town hall) amongst the names and flags in the mosaic pattern that of Stockport can be seen proudly upholding the town's link. Quietly passing this mosaic at frequent intervals are the smart articulated air-conditioned LRVs, modern-day trams which connect Heilbronn via the national railway network with Karlsruhe, used as tram-trains so perfectly suited to a modern transport system.

With its big city neighbour just up the road, and Manchester Airport little more than a stone's throw away, Stockport can also look south and east to the glorious Peak District, whilst who amongst the fair sex will not know of Lyme Hall. and Mr Darcy?

Early 'fifties, before the end of the trams and the big road resurfacing schemes started. A Corporation Crossley climbs Daw Bank and a selection of North Western vehicles share the interest with the pre-war motor cars. *(STA)*

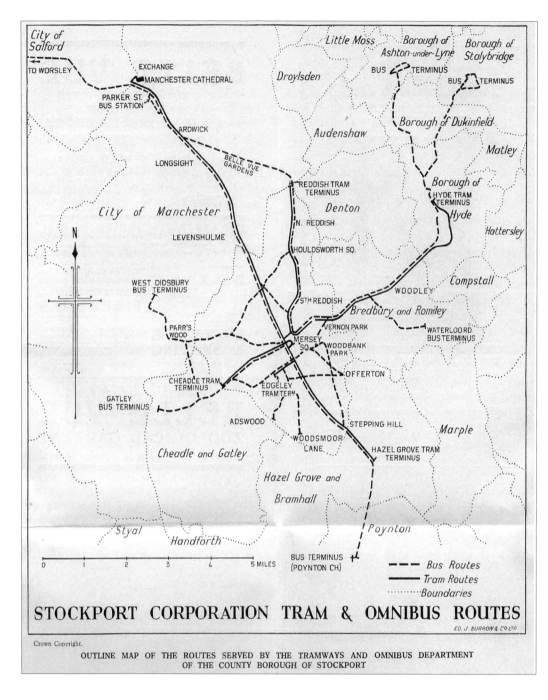

STOCKPORT CORPORATION TRAM & OMNIBUS ROUTES

ED. J. BURROW & CO LTD

Crown Copyright.

OUTLINE MAP OF THE ROUTES SERVED BY THE TRAMWAYS AND OMNIBUS DEPARTMENT
OF THE COUNTY BOROUGH OF STOCKPORT

This official map must date from around 1931/2, for the Gatley tram service which finished in 1931
has been replaced by buses

6

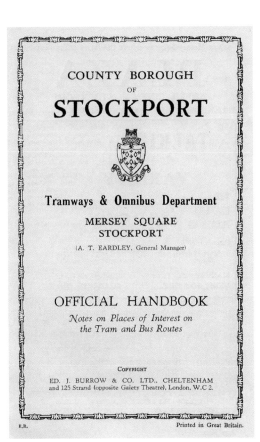

COUNTY BOROUGH

OF

STOCKPORT

Tramways & Omnibus Department

MERSEY SQUARE
STOCKPORT

(A. T. EARDLEY, General Manager)

OFFICIAL HANDBOOK

*Notes on Places of Interest on
the Tram and Bus Routes*

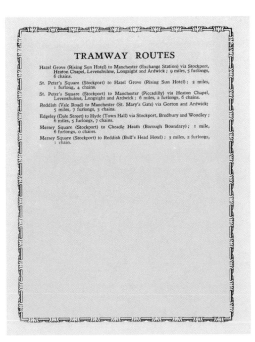

TRAMWAY ROUTES

Hazel Grove (Rising Sun Hotel) to Manchester (Exchange Station) via Stockport, Heaton Chapel, Levenshulme, Longsight and Ardwick ; 9 miles, 5 furlongs, 6 chains.

St. Peter's Square (Stockport) to Hazel Grove (Rising Sun Hotel) ; 3 miles, 1 furlong, 4 chains.

St. Peter's Square (Stockport) to Manchester (Piccadilly) via Heaton Chapel, Levenshulme, Longsight and Ardwick ; 6 miles, 2 furlongs, 6 chains.

Reddish (Vale Road) to Manchester (St. Mary's Gate) via Gorton and Ardwick; 5 miles, 7 furlongs, 3 chains.

Edgeley (Dale Street) to Hyde (Town Hall) via Stockport, Bredbury and Woodley ; 6 miles, 5 furlongs, 7 chains.

Mersey Square (Stockport) to Cheadle Heath (Borough Boundary) ; 1 mile, 6 furlongs, 0 chains.

Mersey Square (Stockport) to Reddish (Bull's Head Hotel) ; 3 miles, 2 furlongs, 1 chain.

MOTOR BUS ROUTES

Mersey Square (Stockport) to junction of Buxton Road and Dialstone Lane via Offerton Fold ; 2 miles, 6 furlongs, 5 chains.

Houldsworth Square (Reddish) to Heaton Moor, Heaton Mersey, Kingsway, and West Didsbury, Manchester (Palatine Road Tram Terminus) ; 5 miles, 1 furlong, 1 chain.

St. Peter's Square (Stockport) to Heaton Mersey, Kingsway, and West Didsbury, Manchester (Palatine Road Tram Terminus) ; 4 miles, 2 furlongs, 6 chains.

Mersey Square (Stockport) to Woodsmoor Lane (Stockport) ; 2 miles, 1 furlong, 3 chains.

Boundary Bridge (Cheadle Heath) to Crossley Road ; 4 miles, 5 furlongs, 0 chains.

Poynton Church to Manchester ; 11 miles, 1 furlong, 0 chains.

Dialstone Lane (Stockport) to Manchester ; 8 miles, 2 furlongs.

Mersey Square (Stockport) to Hyde Town Hall and Stalybridge Station ; 8 miles, 6 furlongs, 5 chains.

Mersey Square (Stockport) to Hyde Town Hall and Ashton (St. Michael's Square) ; 8 miles, 7 furlongs, 1 chain.

Romiley (Waterloo Road) to Manchester, via Stockport and Reddish ; 11 miles, 1 furlong, 7 chains.

Mersey Square (Stockport) to junction of Adswood Road and Garners Lane ; 2 miles, 1 furlong, 3 chains.

Mersey Square (Stockport) to Gatley ; 3 miles, 3 furlongs, 8 chains.

Mersey Square (Stockport) to Borough Boundary (Cheadle Heath) via Woodbank Park, Offerton, Hempshaw Lane, and Shaw Heath ; 5 miles, 1 furlong, 6 chains.

ROLLING STOCK

55 Single Saloon Motor Omnibuses.
85 Double Deck Tramcars.

1 – The Horse Drawn Era

Although we are concerned in this book with local public transport in the streets of Stockport, we must look to neighbouring Manchester for the origins of such transport which would bring horse buses, later horse trams and later still electric trams into Stockport, and indeed beyond, south to the Rising Sun inn at the junction of the Buxton and Macclesfield roads. The latter is, of course, the famous A6 trunk road connecting Scotland with London through Carlisle and its stage coach traffic has already been mentioned in the Introduction.

Despite the protestations au contraire from Londoners, we Mancunians still maintain that horse buses and coaches were operating in Manchester from 1824, thanks to one John Greenwood, keeper of the toll gate at Kersal Bar, pre-dating such transport in the capital and a full five years before Stephenson's Rocket made the news at the Rainhill trials.

Stockport's apparently self-contained transport system, with its always smartly turned out red and white vehicles, is now but a memory and few below the age of 50 will have firm recollections of the system. It is therefore useful to point out that in the tramway heyday – the 1930s – Stockport was situated at the southern end of a huge standard-gauge tramway network which stretched to Hyde and Stalybridge; through Manchester to Oldham, Rochdale, Bolton, Atherton, Swinton, St Helens and Liverpool Pier Head, all with through connections at some stage in their life. Plans which never came to fruition would have linked it with Crewe and Warrington as we shall see. To find out how all this came about we need to go back almost to the mid-19th century.

John Greenwood died in 1851, leaving his son, also named John, in charge of the omnibus undertaking at the age of 33. To compound his problems he now faced competition from a marauding Scot, one G MacEwen, who had the temerity to come south of the border and set up in opposition with a bigger, better and more comfortable form of horse bus. The story (and much more) is told in Ted Gray's masterly history of the Manchester Carriage Company, long out of print but worth searching for in local libraries.

Standing at what would become the Gatley tram terminus, the Horse and Farrier public house, this horse bus shows its depot allocation, L5 for Longsight, but no obvious signs of ownership. The quality of the image, and the style of routeboards, suggests a date in the early 1900s. Is it operating for either Stockport or Manchester to link with the trams? *(MMC)*

MacEwen had a depot in Grey Street, Longsight which later became the base for the Stockport-bound horse trams of the Manchester Carriage & Tramways Company, but, perhaps equally interestingly, survived into the 1980s when its main timbers were rescued for possible use in the construction of a second depot for the preserved electric tramway in Manchester's Heaton Park.

From the above it will be seen that although Stockport could be reached by road from Manchester by stage coach, and then by train from 1843, not until 1880 did the humble tram, which played such a vital role in providing everyday transport for working people, reach the town.

The upshot of all this was that John Greenwood prospered and MacEwen didn't, and their interests were merged into the Manchester Carriage Company Ltd in 1865. Two other events were to influence the direction of the Carriage Company. In 1860 George Francis Train had demonstrated an American-built horse tram in Birkenhead, and ten years later a Tramways Act was passed.

This 1870 Tramways Act decreed that whilst towns and cities might make application to Parliament to build street tramways, and then to construct them, they may not operate the lines themselves. Only Huddersfield became exempt from this ruling simply because the local terrain was so difficult, and the prospect of making any money out of operating a tramway so slender, that no-one would take on the task.

The first horse tramway in the Manchester area opened in May 1877, the line having been built by Manchester and Salford Corporations, with the lease having already been let to Messrs Busby & Turton. However, just before the tramway commenced operation these gentlemen secretly came to an agreement with the Manchester Carriage Company Ltd to operate it, which was not what the Councils had intended or expected.

Since Manchester had decided to construct the lines within the boundary, Busby and Turton had turned their attention to the areas immediately outside Manchester, obtaining powers – together with John Greenwood and Benjamin Whitworth – in 1878 as the Manchester Suburban Tramways Company.

This busy scene at St Mary's Gate, Manchester, shows the mixture of horse trams and buses in the 1870s. The nearest tram is double-ended, pre-dating the Eades patent reversible types in the background. The three-horse bus is almost certainly one of MacEwens (see text) – it is wider than the trams and note that whereas the tram, running on steel rails, required only two horses, a third was required for the bus running over the uneven road surface. The tram turning to head up Market Street could well be heading for Stockport. The horse bus pulling away from the kerb is similar to the one preserved in the Boyle Street, Manchester, Museum of Transport whilst an Eades double-decker tram can be seen at Manchester's Heaton Park tramway. In the distance, Cromwell keeps a fatherly eye on matters. *(STA)*

Back in Manchester, Greenwood's Carriage Company aimed to develop a substantial network of routes which Manchester had promoted and had built, or was building, radiating from the centre of Manchester from 1877, running west to Peel Green, north east to Oldham, north west to Swinton and Pendlebury, east to Ashton and south to St Peter's Square, Stockport, terminating at the Manchester boundary.

At this point all these powers came together with the passing of the Manchester Carriage & Tramways Act of 1880 which combined Greenwood's Company with that of Busby and Turton, vesting in one company powers to operate from the centre of Manchester to Stockport.

The Manchester Carriage & Tramways Company's route mileage reached its peak of 143 miles in the late 1890s. There were over 500 horse trams and a stud in excess of 5,200 horses, 26 horse-buses and 71 horse-drawn cabs in the fleet housed in 19 depots spread throughout the system, all being used to service this extensive mileage.

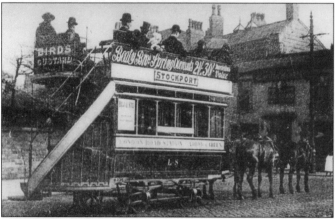

The original Eades cars were fitted with back-to-back seating (known as 'knifeboard' type) on the upper-deck, but later cars were fitted with forward-facing 'garden seat' type accommodation. The cars were lettered along the waist panels as can be seen in these two illustrations – **Levenshulme - Heaton Chapel** on the upper illustration and **London Road Station - Ardwick Green** on the centre one. These would be the terminal points when the cars were short working, but intermediate points when they were used on the full service to Stockport, as in both pictures. The slip board **STOCKPORT** is the key one, showing the ultimate destination.

The Manchester Transport Museum Society has patiently restored to full working order the remains of one of these cars which was discovered in use as an add-on to a wooden hairdresser's shop at Woolley Bridge, Glossop. Whether it came from the Stockport & Hazel Grove Company, or Manchester Corporation to operate in Ashton in c1904, is still being investigated.

The lower picture, taken in March 2008, shows the method of turning the car body without detaching the horse, and eliminating the need for the second staircase. This design reduced the weight of the body and increased the space and carrying capacity for passengers. Turning the car requires quite a deal of space and the routine became unpopular with the police who later banned the whole on-street procedure. Car L53, which operated from Longsight and ran to Stockport, is the only surviving complete Eades car in the world. *(EGC, top, centre; JAS lower)*

In 1880 the Manchester Carriage & Tramways Company – a statutory company and hence not Limited – thus became the operator for horse drawn operation from central Manchester to the boundary at Lloyd Road, Levenshulme and from there along the A6 Wellington Road to St Peter's Square, Stockport, although the two sections had been built and financed separately.

By extending the existing line, this created a double-tracked through route to Manchester's Piccadilly and Cathedral termini from Wellington Road, Stockport. This was opened in April 1880 and, as stated, was worked from the company's Longsight depot by Eades patent double-decked cars built by them in their Ford Lane, Pendleton works, the name coming from their designer and holder of the Patent, John Eades.

Between 8:00am and 10:15pm a basic 15 minute service was operated to Manchester, a journey taking one hour, being augmented in

An interior view of the cars' stabling point behind the Crown Hotel, while, below, we see two reversible horse cars, with their distinctive single-staircase bodywork mounted on a turntable which allowed it to be rotated at termini, avoiding the need for uncoupling the horses in busy streets. Both would have come from the Manchester Carriage Company's fleet but are now owned by the Stockport & Hazel Grove Tramway & Carriage Company Ltd. This view was taken between 1901 and 1905, after which the service ceased and electric trams took over. (MMC; *STA*)

stages along the route by the addition of extra cars, until the section between Ardwick Green and Piccadilly boasted a one-minute service in busy times. Such was the intensity of operation that considerable congestion was caused and this was partially alleviated by running some services down Market Street to Manchester's Cathedral terminus, usually referred to as 'Victoria'. Speed was restricted to 6mph in busy sections, 8mph elsewhere.

There was, of course, a need to cater for traffic south of St Peter's Square and to meet this the Stockport and Hazel Grove Carriage and Tramway Company Ltd was formed in 1889. It financed and built a line from St Peter's Square to Hazel Grove, terminating at Torkington Road some half-a-mile short of the Rising Sun, and this was opened to traffic on 4th April 1890. A branch via Greek Street terminated at Dale Street, Edgeley.

The Company used 16 second-hand trams, mainly Eades double-deck cars purchased from the Carriage & Tramways Company, but at least one Starbuck double-ended car which would have been ordered by Busby and Turton way back in 1877. There were also some single-deck Eades cars and a covered toastrack, together with one of MacEwen's horse buses. This somewhat unlikely assortment was housed in premises behind the Crown Inn at the Junction of Dialstone Lane.

The Company was managed by John Daniels with his brothers Harry, Alfred and Bill acting as conductors. The horses were evidently bought in Ireland by John Daniels.

In Affectionate Remembrance
OF THE

Hazel Grove Horse Cars

Which Succumbed to an
ELECTRIC SHOCK
JULY 5th, 1905.

After many years of faithful Service.

"GONE, BUT NOT FORGOTTEN."

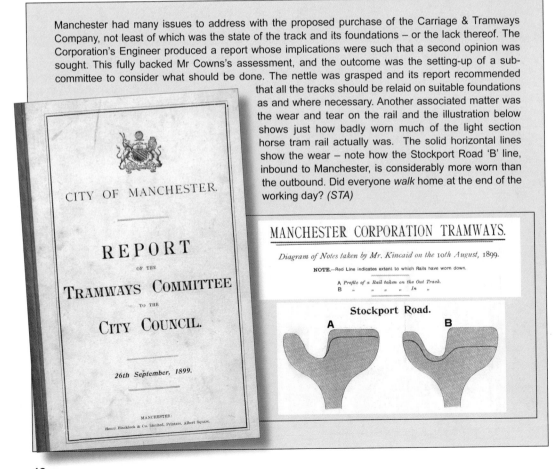

Manchester had many issues to address with the proposed purchase of the Carriage & Tramways Company, not least of which was the state of the track and its foundations – or the lack thereof. The Corporation's Engineer produced a report whose implications were such that a second opinion was sought. This fully backed Mr Cowns's assessment, and the outcome was the setting-up of a sub-committee to consider what should be done. The nettle was grasped and its report recommended that all the tracks should be relaid on suitable foundations as and where necessary. Another associated matter was the wear and tear on the rail and the illustration below shows just how badly worn much of the light section horse tram rail actually was. The solid horizontal lines show the wear – note how the Stockport Road 'B' line, inbound to Manchester, is considerably more worn than the outbound. Did everyone *walk* home at the end of the working day? (STA)

CITY OF MANCHESTER.

REPORT

OF THE

TRAMWAYS COMMITTEE

TO THE

CITY COUNCIL.

26th September, 1899.

MANCHESTER:
Henry Blacklock & Co. Limited, Printers, Albert Square.

MANCHESTER CORPORATION TRAMWAYS.

Diagram of Notes taken by Mr. Kincaid on the 10th August, 1899.

NOTE.—Red Line indicates extent to which Rails have worn down.

A *Profile of a Rail taken on the Out Track.*
B " " " " In "

Stockport Road.

A   B

2 – Towards Electric Traction

On 3rd May 1898, mindful of the need to take action to enable the city to plan for the introduction of electric tramcars onto its streets, Manchester called a conference of surrounding councils to discuss their plans to take over the Manchester Carriage & Tramways Company (MC&TCo) whose many horse-drawn vehicles operated widely throughout the region and whose various 21-year leases were due to expire in the period 1899-1901.

The MC&TCo was now an extremely large organisation as has just been seen, and would be valued at over one-third of a million pounds when the settlement was eventually made – at least £23 million in today's money depending on the yardstick applied. Matters were further complicated by the fact that some lines – usually those outside the Manchester boundary – were actually built, financed, owned and operated by the MC&TCo, and they held the Parliamentary Powers to operate over them. On the other side of the coin, once the electric trams were introduced their assets would be worth very much less, in some cases virtually nothing.

In order to facilitate matters regarding the agreement as to value and subsequent purchase

of all or parts of the MC&TCo, Manchester offered to act on behalf of those local authorities who were involved. Some took advantage of this, others preferred to handle their own affairs.

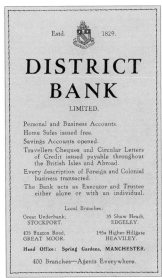

(STA)

A lucky shot, or carefully recording an important scene? Probably the latter as the new Manchester tram poses alongside the Hazel Grove-bound horse tram in St Peter's Square, Stockport. It was taken in 1902 soon after Manchester's electric cars reached the town, but it would be another 20 or so years before Stockport's cars could reach Manchester due to the complicated boundaries and various leasing agreements pertaining at the time. *(MMC)*

3 – Stockport Corporation Tramways

With the Carriage Company's days numbered, and plans being made for electrification in Manchester and elsewhere, it was now time for Stockport to start thinking about placing orders for rolling-stock. Manchester had bought six experimental cars and in November 1899 Stockport was offered the opportunity to inspect these in the former horse bus/horse tram depot in Grey Street, Longsight.

In February 1900 the Stockport Tramways Committee then visited Liverpool, where it was taken with the features of the Bellamy car it was shown, the design taking the name of the General Manager there. Next came a visit to London to the International Tramways & Light Railways Exhibition in the Royal Agricultural Hall at Islington, where the Dick, Kerr stand had an example of that company's version of the Liverpool Bellamy car which again caught the attention of the delegation. They were further impressed to find that both Leeds and Glasgow were taking quantities of this design, Leeds having ordered 100 examples.

Manchester had decided to adopt the short-canopy design which owed much to the former horse trams in the city and which left the driver completely exposed to the elements. Stockport's preference was for the Bellamy design, whereby the extended canopy, with reversed staircases, offered some protection to the driver but, more importantly in those days, provided the facility to carry six additional passengers, three each over the two platforms.

Back in the Council Chambers a period of discussion and assessment followed until, in September 1900, it was agreed that 20 such cars should be acquired, but, mindful of the hilly nature of Stockport's intended system, more powerful motors should be fitted. Accordingly the cars were ordered with 2x35hp units, rather than the 2x25hp of the Exhibition model.

It was decided to build the depot to house this new fleet on the site of the former Mersey Mill, by the river and adjacent to the nascent fire station.

Twenty cars were duly ordered from the Dick, Kerr works at Preston: of these numbers 1-10 had their trolley poles at the side to enable them to pass under the low railway bridge on the proposed Woodley route. (Stockport used only lowheight cars on the Woodley and Hyde route for the entire period of its operation. The cars in later years carried a large 'H' on the dash [H for Hyde] to distinguish them from the remainder of the fleet.)

Consideration was next given to the subject of destination indicators and in 1901 two samples were obtained. One came from The British Electric Car Company, Trafford Park, Manchester and the other from the London Sand Blast Decorative Glassworks. The former was priced at 44/- (£2.20)

August 26th 1901 and Stockport's finest pose at St Marks Bredbury to give their new electric trams a rousing send-off. The first four cars from the new fleet processed in order to Woodley and back.

The cars were decorated as was customary at that time – 1901 was a good year for local potted-palm sellers (and silk hatters!) with the opening of the Manchester (June), Stockport (August), and Salford (October) systems.

Note that no destination boxes are yet carried – the 44/- BEC five-name equipage has still to arrive. *(NDC)*

complete with five destinations, namely, Woodley, Vernon Park, Stockport, Reddish and Cheadle. The price of the unit from the London firm was 54/- (£2.70) so the Manchester firm received the order for indicators for five tramcars. The units comprised metal boxes with rollers and operating mechanisms to take linen blinds 30ins wide with lettering 3¾ins high. Internal illumination was provided and the units were fitted to the balcony rails at each end of the car.

The story now takes an unusual twist, the details varying slightly according to the source. What is not in dispute is that Bolton were already short of trams, for various reasons including late delivery from Dick, Kerr, and according to Bolton records, in 1900 had been offered the loan/hire of four trams ordered by Stockport but for which that system was not yet ready to take delivery. The Stockport version of events is that Bolton returned cars which it had ordered in exchange for 'larger cars', but that is not wholly borne out by the fact that Bolton's replacements were still only four-wheelers, albeit with the six extra seats.

What is also not in dispute is that four trams which operated in Bolton before Stockport opened – as their numbers 41-44 – and differing from other Bolton cars delivered up to then by having extended canopies and reversed stairs, were later returned to the makers and, after refurbishment

and repainting, were delivered to Stockport by April 1902 as its numbers 11-14, with a suitable adjustment to the price of course.

Since this occurred in the period when Stockport was negotiating leases with Manchester, but then leased the tracks to the latter to operate the service as explained earlier, it seems plausible that they may well temporarily have had four surplus cars.

The Department's first office, for the incoming Manager and for conductors to pay in, was situated in Warren Street, by Lancashire Bridge. In 1902 further office accommodation was rented in Brown Street, off what would soon become Princes Street. On 15th May 1901 Mr Hugh McCormick, the first Manager, was appointed, on the same day that the first six trams were delivered (before the opening in August 1901). They were then used for driver training and general route testing. Fellow cars 7-10 were delivered later the same year.

A grand opening ceremony took place on 26th August 1901 in the manner of the time

A gleaming new tram looking quite splendid – but this photograph was clearly posed to show just how badly the reversed staircase impeded the line of sight for the driver; his visibility for anything alongside or behind him was effectively nil. A series of holes were later drilled through one of the staircase risers, but, of course, he had to turn round to see through them, and if anyone was standing on the stairs . . . Note the early form of trolley mast with external springs *(NDC)*

The short-lived Warren Street office, later to be a barber's shop on Lancashire Bridge. *(MMC)*

with speeches, luncheon and everything a proud Borough could be expected to provide.

The trams were housed in the new depot at Mersey Square and the following lines were opened on that momentous occasion:-

Mersey Square to Reddish (Sandy Lane)
Mersey Square to Cheadle Heath
Lancashire Bridge to Woodley

On 31st August a short branch line was opened from Lancashire Bridge to Sandy Lane whilst in January 1902 a works car, to act as a water car for sprinkling to wash the tracks and lay the dust in hot weather, and double-up as a snow plough in bad weather, was delivered from Dick, Kerr's works in Kilmarnock, at a cost of £650. Its electrical equipment was identical to the passenger cars and it was numbered 100 as the first works car, thus keeping it out of the passenger car sequence. A horse drawn tower wagon was acquired at this time to give access to the overhead lines for maintenance and repair. Also at this time the cost of the Borough's share of the settlement with the Carriage Company arrived – £6,138.

The tempo was increasing now, and a further ten cars were ordered for delivery in 1902, with the first of these – the 'Bolton' ones – arriving in October of that year and the last of the final six in 1903. Electricity costs were already taking the attention of the department and this batch of cars were fitted with motors which were stated to be more energy-efficient. Stockport insisted on a penalty-clause with reimbursement if the claims were not substantiated.

That same year also saw the opening on 10th April of the splendid and imposing new fire station in Mersey Square, reflecting the expansion of the

County Borough and its increased responsibilities which that expansion imposed, fronting onto the Square and adjacent to the tram depot which was located further back from the roadway, and alongside the river Mersey.

Further new lines were opened in 1902 :-

Lancashire Bridge-Prince's Street-Mersey Sq.

NB. Prince's Street was originally an easterly extension of Heaton Lane until a visit by the Prince of Wales (later King George V) in July 1908.

Mersey Square-Daw Bank-St Peter's Square

The Reddish route was extended to Houldsworth Square in June 1902 and in July 1902 the Woodley route was extended to the Hyde boundary at Pole Bank where it met the BET subsidiary Oldham, Ashton & Hyde Company's tracks. In August 1903 the Cheadle Heath route was extended to Cheadle Green and was further extended six months later to Gatley. The Reddish route reached its final terminus at the Bulls Head in November 1903.

By this time track brakes had been fitted to the fleet after a couple of run-away accidents with cars unable to stop on steep gradients, of which there was no shortage. One of these involved the water car. The design of lifeguard had also been changed, stemming from the Board of Trade (BoT) Inspector's refusal to accept the type fitted when new. The Committee had visited the Potteries tramways to inspect their lifeguards and in due course settled on the Tidswell equipment.

There had been concern about Manchester's cars using the steep climb up Daw Bank – 1 in 12 – and the Inspector had required track brakes to be fitted. Manchester agreed, but apparently continued to run before the cars had been fitted with the necessary slipper brake equipment, passengers being obliged to get out and walk up the Bank – people power then took over, with passengers refusing the walk up the hill. Manchester took the insurance risk and the BoT evidently turned a blind eye until all the cars were air-braked and compliant.

The year 1903 also saw the introduction of joint operation, something which was to be an important feature of transport operations in the Greater Manchester area for many years. Through cars commenced from Manchester to Stockport (operated at this time only by Manchester), and also from Stockport to Hyde operated by Stockport jointly with cars from BET company The Oldham, Ashton and Hyde Tramway Company whose cars were kept in a small depot in Denton. This former BET subsidiary would later be purchased by the Stalybridge, Hyde, Mossley and Dukinfield Joint Tramways and Electricity Board, a consortium of four local authorities, and commonly referred to as the SHMD Board. In 1904 the cost of traction electricity again raised its head and consideration was given to using the Raworth Patent Regenerative system but nothing came of the idea, perhaps fortuitously in view of events elsewhere, particularly in Rossendale. During October 1904 the foundation stone for the new Town Hall on Wellington Road was laid – the building was opened in July 1908.

Mr Hugh McCormick had been the Tramways Manager since May 1901 but he was dismissed, for reasons believed to have been connected with 'the Stores Book not being in order'. His successor, Mr AT Eardley, was appointed Tramways Manager on 29th January 1904, from 100 applicants, at a salary of £300 per year.

However, the appointment was not without controversy, for certain members of the Council considered that, whilst Mr Eardley was an experienced committee clerk in the Town Clerk's department, he lacked experience with electric tramway traffic. *(One might ask just how many people in 1904 did have such experience!)* An amendment against the appointment was carried by 19 votes to 7. Arising from this there were verbal resignations from those members of the Tramways Committee who had voted in favour of Mr Eardley, including the Chairman, who was also Mayor. A special meeting of the Committee including those members who had resigned was held on 6th February 1904 at which Mr Eardley was again appointed Manager. At this meeting, the Mayor was instructed to call a special meeting of the Town Council for 10th February 1904, to either ratify the decision of the Tramways Committee or appoint a new Tramways Committee. At this meeting the appointment of Mr Eardley was confirmed but at a salary of £250 per year. The recommendation of the Tramways Committee proved to be a good one because Mr Eardley served as Manager for 32 years.

It was around this time that the Warren Street office was closed and its functions were transferred to an office in the car sheds.

The Stockport & Hazel Grove Tramway & Carriage Company Ltd was still operating horse-drawn trams, but as part of the on-going

The Horse and Farrier again, but now the trams have arrived. Number 25 displays the advert panels which in many people's opinion gave the trams more character, as well as bringing in revenue. The advertising contract ran from 1902 to 1907 and this photograph was taken in 1905 – probably to mark the previous year's opening of that section. *(MMC)*

Bolton number 42 bound for Breightmet in early 1901, before being sent back to Dick, Kerr's Preston works for refurbishment and deferred delivery to Stockport as recorded in the text. *(DS)*

preparations for electric traction throughout the Borough, Stockport bought the company on 24th January 1905. The Corporation wasted no time in preparing to make the track suitable for electric cars and it was announced on 11th February that a tender in the sum of £5 12s 6d per ton had been accepted for the supply of rails for the project. The following week it was announced that the tender of RW Blackwell and Co Ltd had been accepted for overhead equipment at a cost of £4,343. The tender of British Thomson-Houston Ltd was accepted for the supply of ten tramcars for the service. Approval was received from the Local Government Board for permission to borrow £30,460 for the reconstruction of the Hazel Grove tramway within the Borough, £9,691 for the construction of the tramway for Edgeley and £1,480 for overhead equipment in the Hazel Grove district. At this time the Tramways Committee decided to tender for the carriage of mail between Stockport and Hazel Grove though nothing came of this initiative.

Work commenced on 13th April 1905 on the reconstruction of the tramway between Stockport

and Hazel Grove with a suitable ceremony after which Councillor Fernley, Chairman of the Tramways Committee, entertained members of the Committee, officials and others at the Warren Bulkeley Hotel. In June 1905, in anticipation of the changeover, the Tramways Committee decided to sell all the horses and tramcars taken over from the Hazel Grove Tramways Company.

In 1905 the next batch of cars, 31-40 arrived to work the Hazel Grove and Edgeley routes as shown on page 21. Unlike all previous cars they came from the Brush Company's works in Loughborough. Originally open-topped, they would be fitted with balcony tops in 1907/08.

The line was reopened using electric cars on 5th July 1905 and later extended from Torkington Road to the Rising Sun in October 1911.

In 1906 the first balcony top-covered cars to be delivered new as such joined the fleet, their numbers following on the sequence as 41-45. They had a three window upper-deck saloon, matching the pillar spacing of the lower deck, and open balconies with conventional 180° staircases.

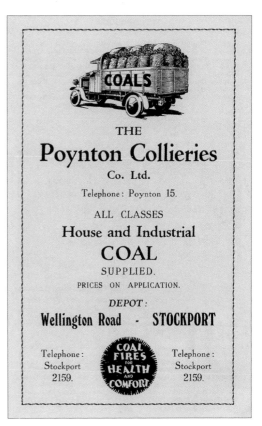

THE

Poynton Collieries
Co. Ltd.

Telephone: Poynton 15.

ALL CLASSES

House and Industrial
COAL
SUPPLIED.

PRICES ON APPLICATION.

DEPOT:

Wellington Road - STOCKPORT

Telephone:
Stockport
2159.

COAL
FIRES
FOR
HEALTH
AND
COMFORT

Telephone:
Stockport
2159.

In 1904 proposals were laid before Parliament for a Mid-Cheshire Tramway, a 3ft 6in gauge line which would have linked Crewe and Warrington with Stockport at Poynton. The ambitious scheme took in the proposal to build a power station and depot at Poynton, and to use the coal from the Poynton collieries to fuel the generating station.

The scheme was abandoned but the advertisement above serves as reminder of the existence of the Poynton collieries. *(STA)*

The splendid panoramic view, left, shows the foot of Wellington Road South, with a Stockport car crossing into Princes Street before the corner was remodelled many years later after demolition of the property dividing Princes Street from Mersey Square in 1935. In the background a Manchester Corporation 4-wheel car makes its way through the Square before climbing Daw Bank to St Peter's Square.

When Manchester introduced its big fleet of bogie enclosed cars – the 'replacement' cars – those working to Stockport terminated in the Square, for they lacked the track brakes required by the BoT to climb the bank.

By 1907 the equally busy Greek Street junction had been fitted with an automatic point turner, speeding up operation and increasing safety for all concerned as traffic increased. *(MMC)*

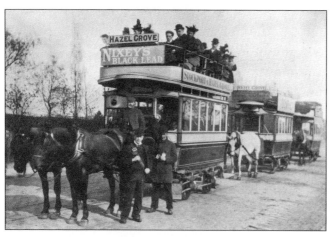

Three of the Stockport & Hazel Grove Tramway Company's fleet of Eades cars, with, presumably, the three Daniels brothers. The advertisement for Nixeys Black Lead will remind older readers of folklore concerning locals blackleading the tramlines. *(MMC)*

Adverts such as the one on the right were commonplace at this time as horse tramways throughout the land were converted to electric traction. Business must have been slow, however, for the Tramways Department was able to buy back two horse cars to convert to salt cars and snow ploughs – one in October and the other in February of the following year. *(STA)*

Claiming to be of the last horse tram to Hazel Grove, this picture would have been taken in the Spring of 1905. *(MMC)*

Brand new Brush-built tramcar number 38 purchased in 1905 for the new Edgeley and Hazel Grove routes stands in Wellington Road South by the turn out from St Peter's Square and facing towards Mersey Square, with the blind showing Hazel Grove during the temporary reversal arrangements linked to the track alterations. In the left hand middle distance the shape of the gasometer which would be demolished to make way for the Heaton Lane complex can just be discerned. The car would be top covered as shown overleaf some two years later. (MMC)

Decorated trams were very much a feature of Edwardian England, and opening ceremonies, Royal visits and the like provided the opportunity for some splendid artistic work. Stockport decorated three open top trams in 1904 to mark the laying of the foundation stone for the new Town Hall. In 1908, to mark the opening ceremony of the completed building by their Royal Highnesses, the Prince and Princess of Wales, the above balcony car was suitably dressed – the practice may well have reflected the naval traditions of dressing a ship overall, at a time when the British Navy was a force to be reckoned with and a source of great national pride. The staircase handrail, with its distinctive shape – nicknamed the trombone for obvious reasons – marks this car as a Brush-bodied BTH product and thus one from the batch 31-40. The extension of Heaton Lane across Wellington Road was then renamed Princes Street to further celebrate the visit. *(MMC)*

George Cardwell was apparently told that this photograph was taken when Frank Clayton and his team were taking a group from one of the local Sunday Schools to some nearby attraction, setting off from the *Jolly Sailor* at Marple where the vehicles were housed. Everyone certainly looks happy in this view on what was clearly a lovely sunny day.

The bus is one of the two Swiss Bernas, though it may have been assembled in England by the British agent Henry Watson & Sons of Newcastle, and marketed as a British Berna. The photograph was taken on Dan Bank, Marple, soon after the bus was delivered in 1910. *(WWC)*

4 – The First Motor Buses arrive in the area – 1908

Stockport's first motor bus route is thought to have commenced around 1908 and was operated by Mr Frank Clayton of Smithy Cottage, Marple Road, using a double-deck open-top petrol driven bus manufactured by Thames Ironworks, Shipbuilding and Engineering Company Limited of Millwall, London. This operated between the Thatched House, Churchgate, Stockport and the Jolly Sailor Hotel, Marple, behind which was his garage.

Mr Clayton employed Mr Arthur Woodhouse of Marple and three London men, Charlie Bean, Charlie Petridge and Alf Sanderson as drivers. Mr Clayton's son Harry also did some driving and conducting but Mr Clayton himself only undertook conducting. During 1910 two Swiss built Berna double-deckers registered DB 219 and DB 224 arrived and later a single-deck Berna was obtained on loan. However, due to financial difficulties the service ceased without warning one Sunday afternoon in July 1912.

Frank Clayton later joined the British Automobile Traction Co as an Inspector when it began operations in Macclesfield in November 1913, becoming an Inspector and a Scheduler before leaving in 1916.

British was operating in a small way at this time but by 1922, as we shall shortly see, it would have a network of services feeding into Stockport.

(In horse-drawn days there was another, unrelated, Clayton family, also working in the same area on the same route, one family apparently operating weekdays and the other weekends, but in competition with each other.)

Following the demolition of the former Mersey Mill adjoining the river, Mersey Square benefited from the construction of the fire station, beyond the tram, and then the tram sheds, out of view on the right behind the bridge. In 1909 the frontage was completed by the opening of the new transport offices, seen at the far end of the bridge. Not until 1929 would the tram depot receive its brick facade as seen in later illustrations. *(MMC)*

In 1910 three-year old balcony car number 49 became the next to be decorated, this time more sombrely, and marking the death in May of that year of King Edward VII. It was photographed at Woodsmoor Church with a suitable entourage of passengers and onlookers. Standing passengers and the decorations on the windows hide the fact that the lower deck seating is now of the transverse 'tip-over' type. *(MMC)*

This 1915 built Dennis tower wagon, registered DB 1123, and purchased through a War Office permit, was the first motor vehicle the department acquired. With typical Ministry efficiency the tower, which was being supplied from Rawlinsons in Manchester, was not made available until 1917 due to pressure of war work at that firm, and the chassis was used for internal coal movement to the electricity department's generating station before being able to be used for overhead line maintenance and repairs as was originally intended. In due course it acquired pneumatic tyres and covered bodywork as seen later in the book. *(MMC both)*

It appears that water car number 100 became the second car to run away, in this case down Lancashire Hill, and as early as June 1902. The department quickly decided to fit air operated track brakes to the car, bringing it in line with the first ten passenger cars which had also been so treated, following a runaway in September 1901, only a few weeks after the opening of the system. Here we see number 100 in later years acting as a mobile recruiting base for the army during the First World War. *(MMC)*

5 – The Trackless Trolleybuses – 1913-1920

The development of the tramway system was now virtually complete and there was a period without expansion until 1911 when the Corporation turned its attention to the expanding Offerton suburb and, further along the road, the small town of Marple.

The area between Offerton and Marple was then, and for many years later, quite rural and clearly offering little in the way of traffic, but Marple itself was apparently considered to be a worthwhile target from which to bring people into Stockport. Expansion of the tramway system to serve these areas was contemplated but was ruled out on the basis of cost and it was decided instead to have 'trackless trolleybuses' where the estimated cost of a system was £800 per mile compared to £5,000 per mile for a tramway.

Towards the end of June 1911 visits were made to Leeds and Bradford, where the first trackless

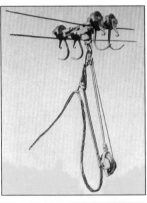

system in the country had been inaugurated on the 20th of that month, and also to Bremen in Germany where the trolleybuses used the 'Lloyd-Kohler' system.

The British Patent rights were taken up by Brush Electrical Engineering of Loughborough who then looked for potential customers. Since Stockport became the only UK user of the system, and mindful that various conflicting reports have been published over the years, we have tried in this volume to set the record straight, partly from contemporary material loaned by Geoff Lumb.

The Lloyd-Kohler system (also known as the Bremen system) used a pair of traction wires mounted one above the other and attached to poles at the side of the road as shown in the illustration below, or attached to the scroll work of lightweight poles. There was only one set of wires for the Offerton route and the 'overhead' carried small four wheeled trucks known locally as 'monkeys' which were connected to the vehicle's bulkhead by a flexible cable.

This meant that when vehicles travelling in opposite directions met, the monkeys had to be unplugged and exchanged between them. Since unplugging the live cable from the vehicle would disconnect the supply, presumably leaving it in darkness, exchanging monkeys at night must have been – to say the least – interesting. In wet weather it must have been hair-raising. The supposed main advantage of the system was that capital costs were lower than those for a conventional system due to there being only one set of overhead lines, and no span wires or bracket arms would be required.

It should not be confused with the Cedes-Stoll system which also originated from Germany, via Austria where it was known as the Mercedes-Stoll system, the name giving the clue to its origins. It became the more popular of the two in this country, with two operators choosing it for their trolleybus systems as opposed to Lloyd-Kohler's

The basic difference between the two German systems was that whereas the Cedes-Stoll version utilised wires side-by-side and suspended above the vehicles, either from span wires or bracket arms (upper illustration), the Lloyd-Kohler method was to attach the wires to poles at the roadside, with one wire directly above the other, though with a suitable space between them. Some modern-day travelling cranes in factories still use this method of current collection. The arrangement was for the positive wire to be in the lower position, enabling the neutral to additionally act as a guard wire. Where the trolleybuses operated away from tram routes special lightweight lattice poles were used to hold the wiring, and similar poles could be found in Keighley for the Cedes-Stoll system operated there. (*GLC; STA*)

one! A company was set up in this country, based in London – Cedes Electric Traction Ltd – but it was forced into liquidation during the First War when the British Government refused to accept it as a British company, regarding it as an alien organisation which was prohibited from trading. Ironically this caused more problems than the spares shortage experienced by Brush for its system since more vehicles were involved.

The line of the proposed route was planned to run through the urban districts of Hazel Grove & Bramhall, and then Marple, where both sets of councillors apparently viewed the notion favourably, and clearly had grandiose visions of great traffic potential and healthy profits, with Marple specifying the Jolly Sailor (the terminus of Frank Clayton's motor bus service and where he garaged his buses between 1908 and 1912 when he withdrew) as the line's terminus.

Stockport wanted the roads brought up to standard and then to be maintained by the UDCs; the latter wanted none of that – but a share of the profits! Marple then decided it wanted the location of the terminus moved to the council offices and Hazel Grove & Bramhall wanted a Joint Committee to oversee fares and stages. Stockport soon grew tired of all this nonsense and curtailed its Parliamentary Bill to terminate the line in Offerton, a distance of around a mile-and-two-thirds from St Peter's Square.

The potential problems of running lightweight electrical vehicles along poorly surfaced roads were recognised and, accordingly, much of the route was surfaced with macadam, the first such in the Borough, and at the tramway department's expense.

Ramsbottom Urban District Council, and Oldham and Ashton Corporations all experienced trolleybus bodies being shaken apart by travelling over setts. Perhaps if they had taken similar precautions to Stockport, the problems would not have occurred?

The operational problems can perhaps be imagined, even on a lightly used road, but just to add to the excitement in Stockport, the meeting point where the monkeys would be exchanged was at the top of a hill. Thus if the crew members were not careful they could lose a monkey which would then run away down the hill needing to be pursued hot-foot by that same crew. It is on record that on more than one occasion the contraption ran all the way down hill to enter the tram shed in Mersey Square, at the foot of Daw Bank, and where the pioneering vehicles were housed.

On 9th October 1911, three trolleybuses were ordered from the Brush company of Loughborough at a cost of £682 each, considerably more than a tramcar on a pounds-per-seat basis and reflecting the pioneering nature of the operation, together with the cost of importing components from

Trackless trolleybus number 2, seen when still quite new at the Offerton terminus with its proud conductor. (PPC)

Waiting patiently outside the Victoria Hotel on Hall Street, number 3 is ready to exchange its monkey with the inbound vehicle as seen on page 30. No tarmacadam here, but note the open lattice-type poles to support the 'overhead' wiring. Where traction poles for the trams existed those were used instead. *(NDC)*

Germany. Each 22-seat vehicle was powered by a 35hp motor and weighed just under four tons. The chassis were Daimler CC types, suitably modified by Brush in their works. The controllers were of tramcar type but developed for foot operation.

The line ran from St Peter's Square, along St Petersgate, Market Place, Churchgate, Spring Gardens, Hall Street and Offerton Lane. When complete the system was inspected on behalf of the Board of Trade by Colonel Von Donop and Mr Trotter, his electrical assistant, on 3rd March 1913. Operations began on 10th March 1913, from Mersey Square to Hempshaw Lane, Offerton.

Not only did the type of overhead system cause problems, but there were issues with the trolleybuses. The main vehicle difficulty was evidently that the back axles were inadequate for the job demanded of them, and new axles did nothing to improve the situation. Then there were complaints about speeding and these led to the route being cut back to Banks Lane in 1915. The complaint about speeding, and the recurring back axle problems, suggest that these vehicles may have been quite sprightly and that the powerful torque from the 35hp motor may have exceeded the designed capability of the differentials and back axles or half shafts.

In 1916 the most troublesome bus, number 1, was sold to the Mexborough & Swinton Tramways Company for £600, a very creditable achievement if it was such a liability and had only cost £682 when new three years earlier. Mexborough already had three similar Brush-built vehicles, though with conventional trolleybooms for overhead wiring, and number 1 became number 24 in its new home. The high price realised reflected scarcities being experienced by that time during World War I; also it should be remembered that Mexborough was part of the large National Electric Construction Company's empire where the necessary know-how and resources to keep these machines in working order would have been more readily available. Be that as it may the new 24 and its three compatriots ran only until 1922.

Meanwhile back in Stockport the other two continued operating, with increasing difficulty, until April 1919 (although a date of 11th September 1920 for final closure is also quoted). Spare parts were no longer available due to the Government ban on 'trading with companies with connections with the enemy'. In desperation, parts from one bus were then used to keep the other one on the road, clearly reducing the timetabled frequency by 50% at a stroke.

Recognising the seriousness of the situation the Corporation entered into talks with George Cardwell, Managing Director of the new

Photographed outside the Brush Electrical Engineering Company's factory in Loughborough, number 1 clearly demonstrates the method of current collection using the Lloyd Kohler system. A socket under the bulkhead can be unplugged and exchanged with another vehicle 'within 15 seconds with practice' said the promotional material. An inertia-reel cable drum houses an additional 30ft of cable to allow for manoeuvring away from the wires which were strung at the roadside. The 'monkey' on the wires weighed some 12lbs, and the wires were 11ins apart. Note the vehicle has a flat roof in this photograph, with a monitor roof in other views. *(GLC)*

Monkey business as the two drivers prepare to exchange their charges, knowing that a dropped catch will result in a trip back to the depot for someone. Careful scrutiny of the sky will reveal both monkeys in this posed shot taken at the location shown on page 28 on Hall Street. The ornate scrollwork on the pole is noteworthy as also is its lattice construction mentioned in the text.

Some similar poles could be seen in north Wales until the Llandudno & Colwyn Bay Electric Railway replaced some of the worn-out traction poles on its tramway.

The open rear platform is almost certainly derived from tramcar design – Brush were of course major manufacturers of electric tramcars – though some motor bus operators such as Lancashire United and Crosville had vehicles of this configuration. Note that number 1 in this view has a monitor roof whereas in other official views at Brush works (as in the example on the previous page) it clearly sports a flat roof. (GLC)

Every employee was issued with a copy of the Bye Laws and Regulations which were prefaced with this warning. Despite shortages of staff due to the war, instant dismissal was still a very real threat for what we might today consider quite minor breaches of the rules. (STA)

NOTICE.

—※—

All persons employed by the Stockport Corporation Tramways Committee are engaged subject to the due and proper observance and performance on their part of the Rules and Regulations of the Tramways Department contained herein, to such additional instructions as may be issued and published from time to time, to the Board of Trade Regulations and to the local Bye-Laws governing the Tramways.

Any omission to observe and perform the above-mentioned Rules, Regulations and Bye-Laws will render an employee liable to dismissal from the service.

A. T. EARDLEY,

General Manager.

October, 1915.

interloping bus company 'British' which was wanting to gain access to Stockport from its Macclesfield base. Stockport hoped that British would agree to take the service over, and operate it with its single-decker motor buses. In a clear case of the biter-bit Cardwell said he would, but only if Stockport dropped their claims for road reinstatement charges where British buses would be run. (See the next chapter.)

Stockport were not prepared to drop these charges and instead decided to exercise their Parliamentary Powers and become a bus operator in their own right. Despite monetary restrictions on borrowing in the aftermath of the war, which lasted for 12 months after hostilities ceased, they were evidently able to order two AEC motor bus chassis at a cost of £1,000 each with bodies by the British Commercial Lorry & Engineering Co Ltd of Bridge Street, Manchester at a cost of £485 each, on 6th May 1919, hoping that these would arrive before the one remaining trolleybus failed. New vehicles were very difficult to obtain at this time and they were very fortunate to be able to contemplate such speedy delivery.

However, this was not to be, for the rear axle failed yet again on 17th June 1919 and the residents of Offerton were without public transport until the arrival of the motor buses on 8th October 1919. They entered service the following day. With their introduction it became possible for the route to be diverted away from Market Place on market days, something not possible with the trolleybuses of course, and this became a feature of Stockport operations on routes 16, 26, 36 and 38 to Offerton and beyond. However, the buses themselves were not totally reliable, and when one was out of service the remaining trolleybus had to be dragged out of retirement and put back into service. Not until the arrival of the third motorbus (see later) could the trolleybus operation finally be closed down completely.

The two trolleybuses languished in the depot for some time before being disposed of, thus ending the first essay into trolleybus operation in the Manchester area.

This photograph was probably taken around 1918, and shows the two survivors, numbers 2 and 3, in the depot. No wires are visible suggesting they are parked away from the area from which they had normally operated, and number 3 appears to be without wheels, presumably standing on blocks. Stockport must have been hoping to repeat their success in selling number 1 for a good price, but they were to be disappointed. *(NDC)*

6 – The 'British' Buses of the BAT Company

We saw, briefly in the last two chapters, how the 'British' buses were now making their presence felt in the area. Indeed the decision to buy motor buses was forced on the Corporation by the combined unreliability of the trackless trolleybuses and the BAT Company (below) declining to take over the service with its own motor buses as we have seen.

The British Automobile Traction Company was a subsidiary of the mighty British Electric Traction Company (BET) which owned tramways throughout the land, including the local Oldham, Ashton-under-Lyne and Hyde Electric Tramways Company Ltd. Operating buses in the area from its base at King Edward Street, Macclesfield with the name British it was keen to operate into Stockport, a move which did not find favour with the councillors of the Borough. The imposition of road charges forced a retreat since British were not willing to pay such fees, and Stockport would not grant licences unless they did.

British then had a stroke of luck when in response to a national rail strike in October 1919, and under Home Office instruction, Stockport was obliged to licence three routes to the BAT Company – Buxton-Stockport; Macclesfield-Stockport; Warrington-Altrincham-Stockport.

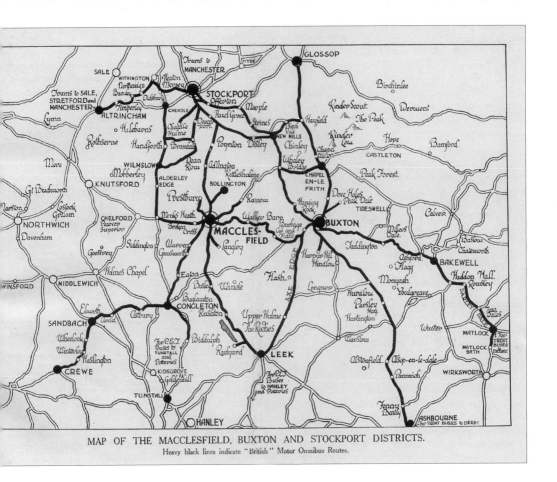

MAP OF THE MACCLESFIELD, BUXTON AND STOCKPORT DISTRICTS.
Heavy black lines indicate "British" Motor Omnibus Routes.

After the strike ended Stockport returned to the *status quo* and British withdrew once more.

British then had to wait until the Road Traffic Act of 1920 came into force on New Year's Day 1921 which abolished the granting of licences being subject to road maintenance charges. British was in at last! Following a new agreement reached regarding services, the Corporation then allowed British Automobile Traction to keep its vehicles in its depot at Mersey Square. Its Stockport address was 1, Mersey Square, something else which must have rankled with those Councillors.

In 1922 the Peak District Committee was formed by British Automobile Traction to administer the services in this area but it was later decided to form a new company and the North Western Road Car Company Ltd came into being on 23rd April 1923. Initially, the registered office was retained at King Edward Street, Macclesfield but later it was decided to move the registered office to Stockport and this was established at Charles Street in 1924. Between 1925-31 a garage and separate workshops were built on one side of the road, and an impressive brick-built office block on the other. This complex eventually housed some 130 of North Western's bus and coach fleet.

This AEC single-decker at the foot of the facing page was typical of the vehicles used by British, the dark green and pale cream livery contrasting with Stockport's red and cream trams. Although this photograph was taken near to the Brush works where the bodywork was built, it is typical of much of the countryside in Cheshire and Derbyshire in which the buses then operated. *(STA)*

The list of services opposite, as at around 1921, gives an idea of the coverage which had already been achieved. *(CMC)*

– and its successor North Western . . .

One of North Western's striking Brush-bodied Tilling Stevens petrol-electric buses is seen in Mersey Square soon after delivery in 1925. It is operating on the former British route to Cheadle. The petrol engine drove a dynamo which produced the electricity for an electric motor which powered the vehicle. Remarkably, one of these fascinating vehicles survives, fully restored, in the Museum of Transport in Boyle Street, Manchester. After withdrawal many passed to fairground showmen who were able to use the dynamo's output to power their attractions. The scene below also dates from the mid-1920s and shows a selection of buses undergoing maintenance and repair in North Western's Charles Street workshops. *(STA both)*

The thick fogs of the first half of the 20th Century, which lasted until the introduction of the Clean Air Act and the gradual closure of the mills and other smoke-emitting factories, created hazards for health and travel alike. On single-track tramways, with passing loops as seen at Pole Bank in the illustration above, it was essential that strict discipline was observed to avoid two cars approaching each other on a single line with almost zero visibility. (Pole Bank Hall is visible on the left.) For clarification drivers were issued with instructions in the form of a printed card, reproduced below. Note the reference to 'Company' cars – those belonging to the Oldham, Ashton & Hyde Company with whom joint operation was maintained until 1921. *(STA; NDC)*

REDDISH AND GATLEY SECTION.

Passing Places in Foggy Weather.

For 7½ Minutes' Service.	For 10 Minutes' Service.	For 15 Minutes' Service.
Gatley Bridge.	Railway Hotel.	Massie Street.
Dr. Godson's Loop.	Vale Road.	Boro' Boundary
Red Lion.	Shepherd's Loop.	Woolpack
Farmers' Arms.	Lancashire Hill	Hotel
Bow Garretts.	Mersey Square.	Lancashire Hill
King Street.	Woolpack	Greg Street
Mersey Square.	Hotel.	Railway Hotel.
Lancashire Hill.	Cheadle Heath	**For 20 Minutes' Service.**
Shepherd's Loop	Station.	
Greg Street.	Queen's Arms Loop.	Queen's Arms Loop.
Vale Road.	Milton	Woolpack H'tel
Houldsworth Arms.	Crescent.	Lancashire Hill Vale Road.
Railway Hotel.		

REDDISH—CHEADLE CARS.

For 10 Minutes' Service.

Railway Hotel.	Mersey Square.
Vale Road.	Woolpack Hotel.
Shepherd's Loop.	Cheadle Heath Station.
Lancashire Hill.	

WOODLEY AND HYDE SECTION.

Passing Places in Foggy Weather.

Stockport Cars must trail Company's Cars between Grapes Hotel and Hyde Town Hall, if foggy, but Cars coming from Hyde must not leave the Grapes Hotel loop until one of our Cars going to Hyde has passed. In the event of current being off on the Company's section, not more than two Cars must go beyond Pole Bank, the other four Cars must maintain the 15 minutes' service between Mersey Square and Pole Bank.

For 15 Minutes' Service.	For 7½ Minutes' Service.
Gt. Portwood Street.	Lancashire Bridge.
Bredbury Bar.	Gt. Portwood Street.
Bredbury Church.	Vernon Park.
Pole Bank.	Bredbury Bar.
Between Grapes Hotel and Hyde Town Hall	Bents Lane.
	Bredbury Church.
	Woodley Station.
	Pole Bank.
	Between Grapes Hotel and Hyde Town Hall

(12/1/15.)

During very foggy weather the safety of the public must be the first consideration.

7 – Other events between 1910 and the 1920s

We have just seen how the trackless trolleybuses came and went, and how the British buses of BAT also came and went, leading to the formation of the North Western Road Car Co Ltd in 1923. We need to take a step backwards now to see what was happening between 1908, when the new Town Hall was opened, and the early 1920s.

In anticipation of running top-covered cars to Gatley it was decided to modify the track layout beneath Wellington Road, interlacing the two lines and moving them nearer to the centre of the arch, thereby creating one of Britain's most famous tram locations with cars negotiating the new track layout whilst being passed above by cars on Wellington Road South.

The following year, 1909, the new Tramways Department offices in Mersey Square were opened and the temporary offices in Brown Street, off Princes Street, which had been in use since September 1902, were vacated. The combination of the new offices and the fire station now gave the square an imposing appearance. It would be some years yet, however, before the actual tram shed was given a suitably matching brick frontage.

The cost of electricity consumed by the trams was again being scrutinised and in 1910 a delegation from Stockport visited the Blackpool, St Annes and Lytham Tramway Co Ltd to see how they were dealing with the situation. This company had installed Ferranti meters on its cars, allowing it to measure the amount of current used by each car on each duty – thus providing a means of comparison against a measured standard. It was common practice to offer drivers a small bonus if they used less than the standard (by coasting) and Stockport decided to adopt the Ferranti meters, and made worthwhile savings as a result.

Following the success of the two batches of balcony top-covered cars now in service, and the public's endorsement of them, it was decided to investigate the fitting of top covers by the Department to the earlier open-top cars in the fleet. Accordingly, visits were arranged to Rawtenstall and Nottingham to inspect the two different types of top covers in use there, and, after due consideration, the Rawtenstall type was selected.

In October 1911 five were ordered from the UEC at Preston, a further ten being ordered in 1912.

The outbreak of war in 1914 led to general unease, and shortages of manpower as many of the staff responded to the call to arms. New rolling stock was virtually unobtainable although the department was able to get a War Office permit to purchase a Dennis motor vehicle, mentioned elsewhere, and which, somewhat by chance, was to have a very long working life. Its intended successor overturned in 1951, leaving the 1915 veteran to soldier on, and to be used to dismantle the overhead when the system eventually closed. Even then its working days were not over, for it spent another five years as a tree lopper.

In September 1915, 310 ornamental pole bases were removed from the traction poles and sent for scrap to help the war effort, whilst another 'recovery' involved the lifting of the unused line down Daw Bank for the rails to be used elsewhere. The following year, in response to the shortage of men, females were employed as conductresses and it may be no coincidence that, acting on behalf of its members, the transport union made a request that the open platform cars should be fitted with vestibules to give some protection against the weather. The Brush company quoted for the work but the request was declined at this time.

Passenger numbers had risen steadily year-on-year, but 1915 showed a small reduction, 11½ million against 12 million the previous year, though mileage was roughly the same at about 1½ million car miles. Eventually the terrible war came to an end, but in a swift indication of the general unrest which was to come there was a national rail strike in 1919.

There was now a great urgency to repair or refurbish the older cars, especially those which had not benefited from the balcony top programme and many of which were in very poor condition.

English Electric, as the Dick, Kerr Company had become in 1919, were consulted and could only offer their standard open top 4-wheel bodies. It was decided to purchase five of these, without the top deck fittings, and to recover top covers from other cars in Stockport's fleet to effect a complicated mix-and-match programme. A bonus was discovered in that these new bottom decks were actually two inches lower than the ones they would replace, enabling the construction of additional lowbridge cars for the Hyde route.

Newly top-covered car 5 seen outside Hyde Town Hall in 1921. After withdrawal the lower deck became a bird watchers 'hide' on the Derbyshire moors above Raworth. It was rescued, painstakingly rebuilt to open-top condition, and since Summer 1996 has been operating on the Blackpool tramway system. Below we see Mr Eardley, with walking cane, and the first of the vestibuled cars, number 29 in 1922. *(MMC both)*

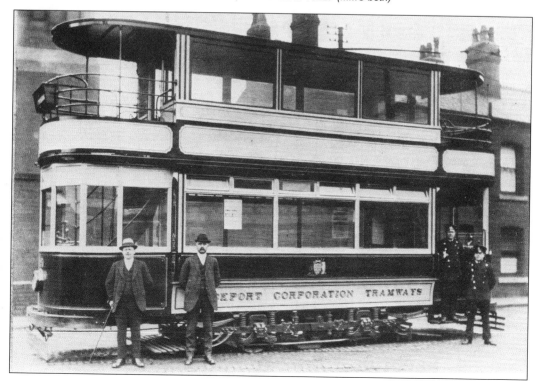

STOCKPORT CORPORATION TRAMWAYS.

OFFICIAL TIME TABLE from 1st December, 1919, and until further notice.

EDGELEY, GEORGE HOTEL (STOCKPORT) and VERNON PARK, BREDBURY, WOODLEY and HYDE.

WEEK-DAYS.

	A.M.	A.M.	A.M.	A.M.	A.M.	A.M.	
Edgeley (Dale St.) d.	..	..	..	..	..	6 37½	And every 15 minutes to 9-52½ p.m. from Edgeley to Hyde and 10-0 p.m. from George Hotel to Hyde. 10-7½ p.m., 10-22½ p.m., 10-37½ p.m. from Edgeley to Woodley only. **Saturdays only** to 10-7½ p.m. from Edgeley and 10-15 p.m. from George Hotel to Hyde. The 10-22½, 10-37½, & 10-52½ p.m., cars from Edgeley only run to Woodley (Pole Bank)
George Hotel, Stockport, or MerseySq	5 20	5 45	6 0	6 15	6 30	6 45	
Vernon Pk & GoytB.	5 30	5 55	6 10	6 25	6 40	6 55	
Bents Lane	5 37	6 2	6 17	6 32	6 47	7 2	
Bredbury Church	..	..	..	..	..	..	
Woodley (Pole B.)(a)	5 45	6 10	6 25	6 40	6 55	7 10	
Hyde Town Hall arr.	..	6 30	6 45	7 0	7 15	7 30	

	A.M.	A.M.	A.M.	
Hyde Town Hall (dep.)	..	..	6 30	And every 15 minutes, Hyde Town Hall to Edgeley to 9-45 p.m. 10-0 p.m., 10-15 p.m., from Hyde to Stockport (Mersey Square) only. **Saturdays only** from Hyde to Edgeley to 10-15 p.m. 10-30 p.m. to 10-45 p.m., 11-0 p.m. from Hyde to Stockport (Mersey Square) only.
Woodley (Pole Bank)	5 45	..	6 45	
Bredbury Church	..	..	..	
Bents Lane	5 54	..	6 51	
Vernon Park and Goyt Bridge	6 0	..	7 1	
Stockport, George Hotel or Mersey Square (arr.)	6 10	6 40	7 10	
Edgeley (Dale Street) (arr.)	..	6 52½	7 22½	

SUNDAYS.

	A.M.	A.M.	A.M.		P.M.	P.M.	P.M.	P.M.	
Edgeley (Dale St.)	...	...	...	And every 30 minutes to 1-0 p.m.	...	...	...	1 52½	Then every 15 mins. to 9-22½ p.m. The 9-37½ and 9-52½ p.m. cars from Edgeley only run to Grapes Hotel (Gee Cross)
George Hotel (dep.)	9 0	9 30	9 30		1 15	1 30	1 45	2 0	
Vernon Park	9 10	9 40	9 40		1 25	1 40	1 55	2 10	
Bents Lane	9 17	9 47	9 47		1 32	1 47	2 2	2 17	
Woodley (Pole Bk.)	9 30	10 0	9 55		1 40	1 55	2 10	2 25	
Hyde T. Hall (arr.)	...	...	1015		2 0	2 15	2 30	2 45	

	A.M.	A.M.	A.M.		P.M.	P.M.	
Hyde T. Hall (dep.)	...	...	10 15	(dep.) And every 30 minutes to 12-45 p.m. from Hyde to Mersey Sq., Stockport.	1 15	1 45	And every 15 minutes from Hyde to Edgeley to 9-45 p.m. 10-0 p.m., 10-15 p.m. from Hyde to Mersey Square, Stockport, only.
Woodley (Pole Bk.)	9 30	10 0	10 30		1 30	2 0	
Bredbury Church	...	...	...		...	...	
Bents Lane	9 39	10 9	10 39		1 39	2 9	
Vernon Park	9 45	10 15	10 45		1 45	2 15	
George Hotel...(arr.)	10 0	10 30	11 0		1 55	2 25	
Edgeley (Dale St.)	...	...	...		2 7½	2 37½	

EDGELEY (DALE STREET), VERNON PARK and BENTS LANE.

WEEK-DAYS.

	A.M.	A.M.	A.M.	A.M.	A.M.	A.M.	A.M.	A.M.	A.M.	A.M.	
Edgeley (Dale Street) (dep.)	6 37½	6 52½	7 7½	7 15	7 22½	7 30	7 37½	7 52½	8 7½	8 15	And every 7½ mins. from Edgeley to Goyt Bridge to 10-15 p.m. from Edgeley See Hyde-Edgeley Section for later Cars.
Stockport (George Hotel or M. Sq	6 45	7 0	7 15	7 22½	7 30	7 37½	7 45	8 0	8 15	8 22½	
Vernon Park or Goyt Bridge(arr.)	6 53	7 10	7 25	7 32	7 40	7 47	7 55	8 10	8 25	8 37½	
Bents Lane (arr.)	7 0	7 17	7 32	7 40	7 47	8 2	8 2	8 17	8 32	...	

	a.m.	a.m.	a.m.	A.M.	A.M.	A.M.	A.M.	A.M.	A.M.	A.M.	A.M.	A.M.	A.M.	
Bents Lane (dep.)	...	...	...	6 54	..	7 9	7 24	7 39	..	7 54	..	8 9	...	And every 7½ minutes between Goyt Bidger and Edgeley to 10-22½ p.m. from Goyt Bridge. See Hyde-Edgeley Section for later Cars.
Vernon Park and Goyt Bridge	...	...	...	7 0	..	7 15	7 30	7 45	7 52½	8 0	8 7½	8 15	8 22½	
St. Peter's Square	6 25	6 40	6 55	7 12	7 17	7 27	7 42	7 57	8 5	8 12	8 20	8 27	8 35	
Edgeley (Dale Street) (arr.)	6 37½	6 52½	7 7½	7 22½	7 30	7 37½	7 52½	8 7½	8 15	8 22½	8 30	8 37½	8 45	

SUNDAYS.

	P.M.	
(dep.)	2 0	And every 7½ minutes to 10-0 p.m. from Edgeley to Vernon Park.
	2 7½	
(arr.)	2 22	

P.M.	
2 17	And every 7½ minutes from Bents Lane to Edgeley to 9-47 p.m. For later Cars see Hyde.—Edgeley Section.
2 22½	
2 35	
2 45	

MERSEY SQUARE (STOCKPORT) and REDDISH (GORTON BOUNDARY).

WEEK-DAYS.

	A.M.	A.M.	A.M.	
Mersey Square (Stockport) dep.	4 50	5 30	6 0	And every 10 minutes from Mersey Sq. to Reddish to 10-0 p.m., then every 15 minutes to 11-0 p.m. Saturdays to 11-10 p.m.
Reddish (Terminus)	5 15	5 55	6 25	

	A.M.	A.M.	A.M.	
Reddish (Terminus) dep.	5 15	5 59	6 25	And every 10 minutes from Reddish to Mersey Sq. to 10-25 p.m., then every 15 minutes to 11-25 p.m. Sat., 11-35 p.m..
Mersey Sq. (Stockport) arr.	5 40	6 20	6 50	

SUNDAYS.

	A.M.		A.M.	
Mersey Square (dep.)	9 30	And every 20 minutes from Mersey Square to Reddish to	1 40	Then every 10 minutes from Mersey Square to Reddish to 10-30 p.m.
Reddish (Terminus) (arr.)	9 55		2 5	

	A.M.		P.M.	
Reddish (Terminus) (dep.)	9 55	And every 20 minutes from Reddish to Mersey Square to	2 5	Then every 10 minutes from Reddish to Mersey Square to 10-55 p.m.
Mersey Square (arr.)	10 20		2 30	

MERSEY SQUARE (STOCKPORT), CHEADLE HEATH, CHEADLE, and GATLEY.

WEEK-DAYS.

	A.M.	A.M.	A.M.	A.M.	
Mersey Sq. (Stockport) (dep.)	5 15	6 0	6 10	6 20	And every 20 minutes from Mersey Square to Gatley to 10 p.m., Sat. 10-40 p.m., and every 10 minutes from Mersey Sq. to Cheadle to 10-50 p.m., Sat. 11 p.m.
Cheadle (arr.)	5 30	6 15	6 25	6 35	
Gatley (arr.)	..	..	..	6 45	

	A.M.	A.M.	A.M.	A.M.	A.M.	A.M.	
Gatley (dep.)	..	..	..	..	..	6 45	And every 20 mins. from Gatley to Mersey Sq. to 10-25 p.m. Sat. 11-5 p.m. And every 10 minutes from Cheadle to Mersey Square to 11-5 p.m. Saturday, 11-15 p.m.
Cheadle (dep.)	5 30	6 15	6 25	6 35	6 45	6 55	
Mersey Sq. (Stockport) (arr.)	5 45	6 30	6 40	6 50	7 0	7 10	

SUNDAYS.

	A.M.		P.M.	
Mersey Square (Skpt.) (dep.)	9 20	And every 20 mins. Mersey Square to Gatley to	1 40	And every 20 minutes Mersey Square to Gatley to 10-0 p.m. And every 10 mins. Mersey Sq. to Cheadle to 10-20 p.m.
Cheadle	9 35		1 55	
Gatley (arr.)	9 45		2 5	

	A.M.			
Gatley (dep.)	9 45	And every 20 mins. Gatley to Mersey Square to	2 5	And every 20 mins. Gatley to Mersey Sq. to 10-25 p.m. And every 10 mins. from Cheadle to Mersey Sq. to 10-35 p.m.
Cheadle	9 50		2 15	
Mersey Square (Skpt.) (arr.)	10 10		2 30	

ST. PETER'S SQUARE (STOCKPORT), CROWN INN, and HAZEL GROVE.

WEEK-DAYS.

	A.M.	A.M.	A.M.	
St. Peter's Sq. (Stockport) (dep)	5 15	5 40	5 54	And every 6 minutes from St. Peter's Square to Hazel Grove to 11-0 p.m. Saturday, 11-10 p.m.
Crown Inn				
Hazel Grove (arr.)	5 35	6 0	6 15	

	A.M.	A.M.	A.M.	
Hazel Grove (dep.)	5 35	6 0	6 15	And every 6 minutes from Hazel Grove to St. Peter's Square to 11-20 p.m. Saturday, 11-30 p.m.
Crown Inn				
St.Peter's Sq. (Stockport (arr.)	5 55	6 20	6 34	

SUNDAYS.

	A.M.		P.M.	
St. Peter's Square (dep.)	9 0	And every 10 mins. from St. Peter's Square to Hazel Grove to 1-30 p.m.	1 42	Then every 6 mins. from Stockport to Hazel Grove to 10-36 p.m. Last Car 10-40 p.m.
Crown Inn	..		1 55	
Hazel Grove (arr.)	9 20		2 3	

	A.M.		P.M.	
Hazel Grove (dep.)	9 20	And every 10 minutes from Hazel Grove to St. Peter's Square to 1-50 p.m.	2 3	Then every 6 minutes from Hazel Grove to Stockport to 10-57 p.m. Last Car 11-0 p.m.
Crown Inn	..		2 15	
St. Peter's Square (arr.)	9 40		2 20	

STOCKPORT (ST. PETER'S SQUARE) and OFFERTON.

WEEK-DAYS.

On Market Days the Route is Via Lord Street and Wellington Street.

	P.M.	
St. Peter's Square, Stockport (dep.)	7 0	And every 30 minutes to 10-30 p.m.
Offerton (Terminus) (arr.)	7 15	

	P.M.	
Offerton (Terminus) (dep.)	7 15	And every 30 minutes to 10-45 p.m.
St. Peter's Square, Stockport (arr.)	7 30	

Sundays.

	P.M.	
St. Peter's Square (Stockport) (dep.)	1 30	And every 30 minutes to 9-30 p.m.
Offerton (Terminus) (arr.)	1 45	

	P.M.	
Offerton (Terminus) (dep).	1 45	And every 30 minutes to 9-45 p.m.
St. Peter's Square (Stockport) (arr.)	2 0	

Care has been taken to ensure the accuracy of the information contained in the table, but no responsibility will be accepted by the Corporation for the consequences of any errors which may appear. The Corporation reserve to themselves power to alter the times or discontinue the running of any of the Cars, and will not be responsible for any loss arising therefrom or from delay or accident.

The 1919 tram timetable. The Offerton service is now shown at 30min intervals; the trolleybuses have supposedly finished to be replaced by buses, but the buses themselves were not completely reliable and the service has thus become half-hourly. *(MMC)*

Stockport Tramways Department was still in charge of its own generating station at this point in time, however in 1919 the Electricity Supply Act was passed and following its implementation the Tramways Department was obliged in 1923 to hand over its generating plant to the Borough Electricity Department. It was the start of the road which would lead, eventually, to the Nationalisation of electricity supplies in 1948, the next step being the connection to the National Grid in 1928. Stockport had always been, and would remain, a very efficient user of power and the loss of control would not have been welcome.

The arrival of the Borough's first motor buses is covered in the next chapter, and Stockport's buses and trams would continue to work side-by-side in harmony for another three decades.

Facing page: The first batch of totally enclosed cars arrived in 1920 in anticipation of the through running to Manchester. They were the first Stockport cars to be fitted with platform doors but local legend has it that the doors' days were numbered after Manager Eardley was left at the stop one evening, being unable to board through the closed doors!

As part of the on-going modernisation routine they also had more comfortable, upholstered, seating and other refinements. The upshot of all this was an increase in weight such that broken axles very quickly became a feature of the batch, and makers Brush were required to fit stronger axles to remedy the problem. *(MMC)*

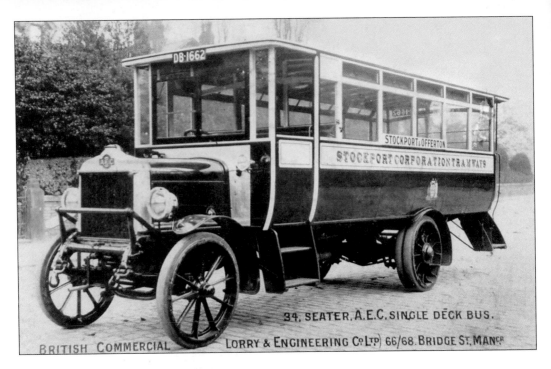

34, SEATER, A.E.C. SINGLE DECK BUS.

BRITISH COMMERCIAL LORRY & ENGINEERING Co LTP) 66/68. BRIDGE ST, MANCR

8 – Stockport's own first Motor Buses now arrive

Stockport had ordered two AEC YC single-decker buses to replace the defunct trackless trolleys, as was mentioned in the previous chapter, and these arrived in October 1919 and were numbered 101/2. A third vehicle was necessary to be able to maintain the service, and by good chance a similar vehicle became available on the second-hand market, being purchased in June 1920 for £1,200 via the auctioneers dealing with the cessation of Kirkburton Motors Ltd of Huddersfield. It was numbered 103 and re-registered as DB 1814.

There were thus now three virtually identical AECs, all fitted with bodywork by the British Commercial Lorry & Engineering Co Ltd of Manchester, that company being AEC's principal dealer in the north of England. In addition to this dealership it also had its own coachbuilding facility in Whalley Range, Manchester, believed to have been located in the former horse tram depot in that suburb which became redundant after the Carriage Company ceased to operate tramcars.

With these three vehicles under its belt the department was able to keep the Offerton residents happy, and also to gain experience of motor bus operation as opposed to trolleybus tribulations.

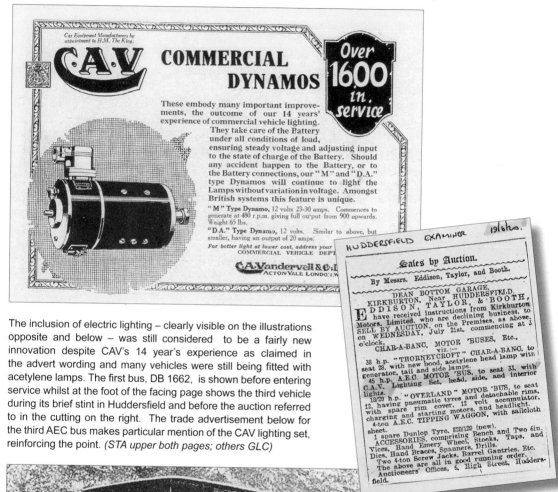

The inclusion of electric lighting – clearly visible on the illustrations opposite and below – was still considered to be a fairly new innovation despite CAV's 14 year's experience as claimed in the advert wording and many vehicles were still being fitted with acetylene lamps. The first bus, DB 1662, is shown before entering service whilst at the foot of the facing page shows the third vehicle during its brief stint in Huddersfield and before the auction referred to in the cutting on the right. The trade advertisement below for the third AEC bus makes particular mention of the CAV lighting set, reinforcing the point. *(STA upper both pages; others GLC)*

9 – Development during the Busy 1920s

Although the Department had been able to take delivery of new trams 51-60 in 1920, and a further batch (66-75) would arrive in 1922, there was much work to be done on repairing the infrastructure. Unavoidable neglect during the war years due to lack of manpower, and restrictions on expenditure and borrowing after the end of the conflict, resulted in a backlog of permanent way and other vital work.

The purchase of more buses was already being considered, but these were seen as small vehicles, carrying around 20 passengers, and either acting as feeders to the trams or operating where there was insufficient traffic potential for trams. Clearly the trams were going to continue to be the prime movers, and much work would need to be done to enhance the system's capacity. However, it was not only the track that was wearing out. The first 30 cars, the open-toppers from 1901-3, were clearly in need of major attention. Some had already been rebuilt and had received top covers but the rest were looking very sorry for themselves. Although the expertise and facilities to rebuild these cars was available in-house a more radical solution was proposed and so, in 1921, it

was decided to purchase five complete lower-deck saloons from English Electric in order to allow this much-needed rebuilding to take place. Further work on other cars meant that a major programme was being initiated and John Eades Jnr, formerly of the Carriage Company and later Car Works Superintendent at Manchester's Hyde Road Works was employed on short-term contract to supervise matters. Although the finished rebuilds, now totally-enclosed, were of low height, it had been necessary to lengthen the truck frames to match these new saloons. The resulting cars were numbered 61-65. Mr Eardley no doubt ensured that the doors also quietly disappeared from his *bete noir* class during this busy time!

Doubling of track layouts to remove passing loops which slowed down the service, equipping cars with high-speed motors and changing gear ratios to increase speed potential were two of the broad strategies employed. Auto-sanders, linked to the braking notches on the controllers, were

One of the Oldham, Ashton & Hyde Company's diminutive turtle back roofed single-deckers – number 15 – photographed in Gee Cross village shortly after the extension of the line to Pole Bank to connect with the Stockport system in 1903. The design was adopted as a BET standard and 25 such cars were built for various of the group's subsidiaries, all on Peckham trucks. *(WGSH collection)*

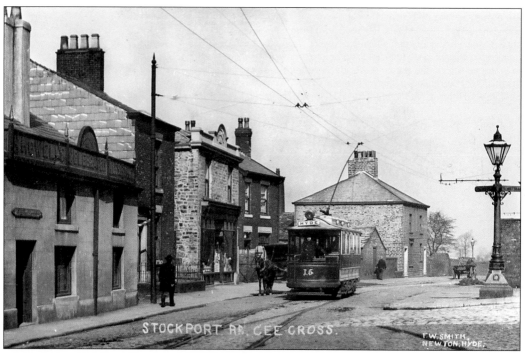

A familiar location, but a less familiar tram. SHMD number 63 was one of the four low height cars built as late as 1924/5 to replace obsolete O A & H company cars for the through route from Hyde to Stockport, and stands in Mersey Square. It was later adopted as the emblem of The Tramway Museum Society. *(NDC)*

also installed in this period to improve braking efficiency commensurate with the higher running speeds. This brought the Department's cars in line with neighbouring Manchester, an important point not least with joint operation on the various workings of the 35 route. By the mid-1920s the trams were busier than ever and this investment had clearly paid off – in 1925 over 27 million passengers were carried, and over 2 million car miles were operated, actual increases of 237% and 140% respectively on a decade earlier.

With the greater number of top-covered cars in the fleet it was now decided to clearly mark those so-called low bridge trams which were capable of passing beneath Bredbury and Woodley railway bridges. This was accomplished by painting a large letter H either side of the headlamps.

During 1921 the Oldham, Ashton & Hyde Tramway Company Ltd was purchased by the local authorities in whose areas it had operated when its 21 year leases expired, and the SHMD Joint Board took over some of its operations, including the service now between Hyde and Stockport. Thus SHMD cars would appear in Stockport. SHMD built four new low height balcony top cars for this service, enabling them to pass under the railway bridges at Bredbury and Woodley.

The OA&H Company was a BET subsidiary, having been formed in 1899, and having a depot

in Denton. Its cars operated two routes, from Ashton to Hathershaw, at the Oldham boundary, and from Ashton to Pole Bank, Bredbury, later cut back to Gee Cross. The green and white livery was similar to that of the SHMD cars, but their appearance was quite distinctive as the photograph (opposite) of one of the single-deckers indicates. Geoff Hyde in his *History of Transport in Ashton under Lyne (TPC 1974)* gives a brief history of the company, and the same author's *SHMD history (TPC 1990)* should also be sought out.

The next significant expiry of leases under the famous 1870 Tramways Act was due in June 1923, that of the tracks to Manchester. Stockport decided not to renew or extend the lease but to operate the service with its own cars, running jointly with Manchester. The work of relaying this main line was also put in hand since the track laid by Manchester in 1901 was now worn out.

There was insufficient room in the Mersey Square tram depot for the extra cars which would be needed for the Manchester service,

and work began in June 1923 to demolish the public weighbridge and realign the track into the permanent way yard, thus allowing the creation of a second depot, in Heaton Lane. A further ten cars (66-75) were then ordered, pending completion of this new facility, after which another ten would be purchased. All would come from Cravens factory at Darnall in Sheffield.

Whilst this tramway development was in progress, the Corporation continued to expand its motor bus services in the borough. A service from Manchester Road to Bank Hall Road, Heaton Mersey commenced in 1922 and was extended to Reddish on 9th May 1923. On 31st March 1924 the original Offerton route was extended to Dialstone Lane with small 21-seat Vulcan single-deckers numbers 104-7 being bought for this purpose from the Southport manufacturer during late 1923. However, it was not a success and was cut back again after a year. A further pair of Vulcans arrived in 1924, this time the larger VSD model with 26-seat dual-doorway bodywork.

The final batch of trams was delivered at the end of 1925 and into January 1926. Numbered 76-85 they took the passenger cars to their highest fleet numbers, with only works cars 100 and its cohorts (up to 103) carrying higher numbers.

Lancashire Hill during the winter of 1923/4, with all the appurtenances of the relaying project – a crane for moving the rail, tar boiler in the distance, a pile of setts waiting to be put back when the job is eventually finished and a generous coating of mud in the cold miserable weather. *(MMC)*

The dual-doorway bodywork on the final batch of Vulcans must have made a good impression – perhaps better than the chassis did – for in 1926 ten new Leyland PLSC1 Lion single-deckers

One of the small Vulcan single-deckers purchased by Stockport in 1923 and numbered 104-7. Two doors on such a small bus might just be thought to be somewhat of an overkill? They had a short life, three being withdrawn in 1927 and the last one in 1929. *(EOC)*

Stockport's motor vehicle experience pre-1920 was fairly limited, with the Dennis motor tower wagon holding the fort until the first of the AEC trolleybus-replacements arrived in October 1919.

In the early post-war days new vehicles were extremely difficult to obtain, and this may explain why the department chose to switch to Vulcans for further deliveries – restrictions on borrowing money were also tight in the aftermath of the conflict.

Vulcan, based in Southport, manufactured its own engine, chassis and bodywork, and the first purchase was the open truck seen below – DB 2649 – for carrying welding equipment for the permanent way department. It was acquired for £900 in November 1920 and is posed here outside the fire station doors – next to the depot.

The two AEC bus chassis (only) had cost £1,000 each and there would thus appear to have been a reasonable saving with the complete vehicle at £900.

The mechanical aspects of the truck must have impressed, orders for passenger vehicles following soon afterwards. Vulcan's range included a 21-seat single-deck bus with normal control, *ie* where the driver sat behind the engine rather than alongside it, as seen in the small illustration opposite. Stockport took four of these during 1923, and then, in 1924, two of the full-size Prince models similar to the drawing in the accompanying advert. The Vulcans lasted only until 1929. *(STA advert; MMC)*

Number 110, DB 6851, seen here before delivery, was the first of the PLSC Lions which made such an impact in the fleet. It carries the Leyland body which became instantly recognisable in fleets throughout the country. *(BCVM L003678a)*

with comparatively unusual Leyland dual-door bodywork were purchased, and a new circular service commenced on 4th January 1926 covering Turncroft Lane-Mile End Lane-Woodsmoor Lane-Cale Green-Greek Street. The Lion was one of Leyland's great success stories and Stockport was just one of many satisfied customers. It would be the satisfaction with this model that would mean that Leyland would become the main supplier to the end of the Department's existence.

In November 1926 two more new routes were established, one to the Farmers Arms and the other via Lancashire Hill to the boundary with Manchester at Lloyd Road, Levenshulme. On 9th January 1927, these routes were joined to form a cross town route which was extended to Cheadle to replace the tram service which was cut back to the boundary. Three weeks later, the inter-urban express service (Chapter 9) between Stockport and Hyde was commenced. September 1927 brought some significant changes. On 3rd the Offerton route was again extended to Dialstone Lane and

Leyland's PLSC Lion model transformed the bus fleet; reliable and comfortable, and capable of much higher speeds than the law allowed, they gave up to 23 years service – compare this to 4-5 years for the Vulcans and, when we come to them, 6 years for the Crossleys. The Lion had a high frame chassis and its Cravens body was unbalanced, with the waistline far too high, giving small windows. The tramcar style indicator box also did little for the appearance. *(STA)*

linked to the Heaton Mersey service to form a cross town service. On 9th both this service and the Reddish service were extended from Heaton Mersey to Kingsway.

Also in 1927 the new Heaton Lane office building was opened. It stood on the site of a former gasworks, fronting onto the main A6 Wellington Road where the gasometer had been a local landmark. When the complex was extended some eight years later, the offices and adjacent bus garage and tram depot, with entrance archway and clock tower, would become an even more familiar, and a much more attractive, landmark. The original Mersey Square tram depot, just across the A6, continued in use.

Soon afterwards two further batches of Leyland Lions were purchased, three with bodywork by Short Bros of Rochester, numbered 120-2 in 1927, and twelve bodied by Cravens of Sheffield (no relation to the Reddish company of the same name), allocated fleet numbers 123-34, in 1928. All were of dual-doorway configuration. Whilst these new buses were taking their place in the fleet upgrading of the trams continued and in this year, 1928, car 81 was experimentally fitted with an 8ft wheelbase Cravens truck. It was so successful that the whole class was similarly equipped in 1929, and then further cars in 1933.

During the Spring of 1929 a visit was made to Lincoln, where the pale green and cream cars on its standard gauge tramway had been withdrawn

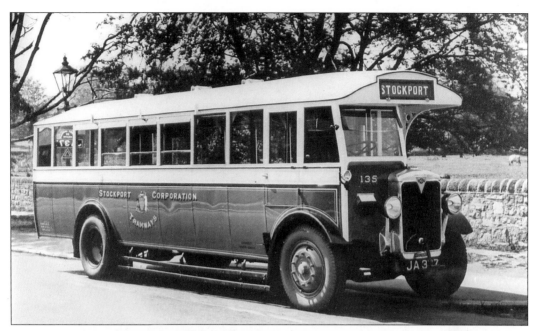

Cravens' workmanship on the trams obviously satisfied, and when they came to body the AEC Reliances, above, they suddenly showed some flair, taking full advantage of the lower chassis frame and also building-in the indicator box – compare the views above with the body they built on the Lions, as seen in the view opposite taken in their works before delivery. Even a small seated passenger would now be able to see through those deep windows. Unfortunately the chassis did not give such service as the Leyland Lions and the first of these 12 AECs was withdrawn as early as 1936, with only one seeing out the war. The last Lion was not withdrawn until 1949. *(STA all)*

on 4th March of that year. Stockport found nothing of interest either in cars, equipment or spares, but Preston took three balcony cars for its system. Stockport's fleet had thus now reached its maximum of 85 passenger cars, and, perhaps acknowledging this fact, Mersey Square depot received a smart brick frontage after an extension to its capacity in 1929.

Turning now to traffic matters, through cars from Stockport began to operate to Gorton library, via Hyde Road from Reddish, in order to serve

The steady increase in numbers of buses in the fleet – 46 by 1929 – necessitated extending the Mersey Square depot to provide accommodation and servicing facilities. Here one of the AEC Reliances stands on the hydraulic lift whilst awaiting routine attention. Note the chassis to the left. *(MM courtesy Chris Heaps)*

the busy Beyer, Peacock railway works there, and also the LNER 'Gorton Tank' railway works across the lines where locomotives and rolling stock were built and repaired. It was at this time that CF Wolsey joined the department as Traffic Superintendent, replacing C Sprowson. Wolsey came from Sheffield Corporation, but his stay was short before he moved on to higher things in the Isle of Man. He would, however, have been in time to see Stockport cars standing alongside both Manchester and Salford cars in Reddish on their jointly operated 33 service to Swinton but, in 1933, it was divided and Salford's cars worked only as far as Deansgate from Swinton. If he was a Stockport County fan he would, perhaps, have taken the opportunity of riding to Edgeley for home games on Saturday afternoons on a Manchester bogie car – purely for research of course. He may also have been made aware of the lightly-trafficked Gatley section, for in 1931 it was cut back to Cheadle.

Whilst this first abandonment would have released just a small number of cars, two of them

were quickly withdrawn – number 7 was partly dismantled and became a static driver-trainer in the depot whilst number 10 was completely dismantled and used for spares.

Back on the bus side of the organisation the next vehicles to be purchased showed a short-lived reversion to AEC, with twelve of the new Reliance model arriving in 1929 and carrying numbers 135-46. Like the last batch of Lions, they carried bodywork by Cravens of Darnall with a further six of the same combination being delivered the following year numbered 147-52.

With this quite significant increase in the size of the bus intake, depot space was again becoming a problem. There were ideas of building a new bus depot out towards Cheadle but a more sensible solution presented itself much nearer to the main offices and Mersey Square depot where further land could be made available by purchasing and demolishing Lieutenant Colonel Wilkinson's mill which adjoined the former gasworks site. The steady decline of the mills was at least providing some benefit in the Borough.

Work began in 1931 and a new bus depot was built behind the 1927 office complex which it will be remembered stood on the junction of Heaton Lane and Mersey Square, 200 yards from the original tram depot and adjoining the 1924-built Heaton Lane five-road shed which now housed 55 of the fleet's tramcars.

The arrival in 1931 of six Crossley Alpha single-deckers, Nos. 153-58, with bodywork by the same manufacturer, was perhaps to be expected, but there were no more from this source until the arrival of the first double-deckers in 1941. Here number 156, JA 1462, is seen working on the 31 service which operated between Stockport, Hyde and Ashton. Maurice Marshall records that this batch also worked the through service to Worsley. They had short lives, all being withdrawn in 1936.

The destination display is identical to some Leyland Tigers delivered to Sheffield around this time; no surprise perhaps to find that Stockport's new Traffic Manager in 1930 was one Cyril Frank Wolsey and that he had just joined the department from Sheffield. Note the Lion, opposite, had no provision for route numbers as built.

In 1932 Wolsey moved to become GM of the Douglas (IoM) Corporation system, later designing the famous destination display on a batch of Guy single-deckers which became legendary as 'Wolsey's Camels'. *(NDC)*

Another 'camel' was the AEC Regent mentioned earlier, and looking similar to the Cornish example below. The demonstrator, carrying fleet number 153 and registered as JA 1291, was tried out in 1930. Bodied by Shorts with their distinctive roofline as seen here, it was returned as unsuitable due to the many overhanging trees and also being under powered – the fleet number was re-issued to the first of the Alphas and the Regent ended up with the Midland General fleet. Tree lopping had yet to become an everyday part of the Department's – and the Borough's – work routine but more double-deckers arriving in 1934 would enforce that change. *(STA)*

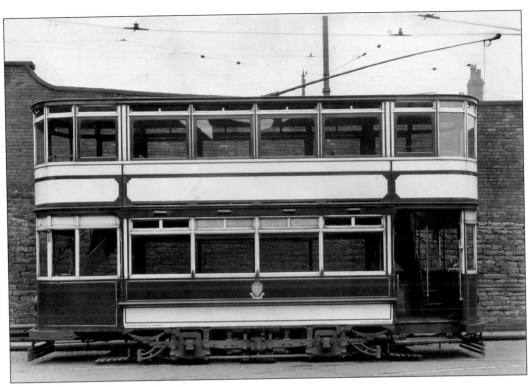

Cars 76-85, (as above), were destined to be Stockport's last trams. Once again built by Cravens, in Sheffield, they incorporated the various refinements that had gradually been built into previous batches, notably the 8ft wheelbase truck for improved riding, the adoption of a more comfortable type of car seating – upholstered in red leathercloth – and, of course, with enclosed vestibules on both decks. The bodywork is again of 4-window construction and sharp eyes will notice the new coat of arms referred to earlier gracing the waist panel. *(MMC)*

Leyland-bodied PLSC1 Lion, number 116, shows the new destination number arrangement and what is believed to be its instigator – Traffic Manager Cyril Frank Wolsey. *(NDC)*

Visiting Tramcars

In addition to trams working into Stockport in the daily course of joint operation from Manchester and Hyde, there were occasional incursions from more exotic vehicles for special events. In 1926 the transport department borrowed the **Shopping Week** decorated car from Liverpool, seen below. It was driven from Liverpool by Inspector GH Reeder, travelling by way of Prescot, St Helens, Atherton, Swinton, Salford and Manchester in a journey which took several hours. It came on 14/11/1926, and toured all routes in the Borough before being returned on 21/11/1926. It thus visited the extremities of the vast south Lancashire standard gauge network and travelled from the outflow of the river Mersey to the source. *(MMC)*

In 1931 this Ashton Corporation single-decker visited Stockport as part of the celebrations to mark the centenary of the discovery of electro-magnetic induction in 1831 by Michael Faraday. Photographed against the wall of Heaton Lane depot the little single-decker stands against a backdrop of brake blocks. The Stockport power station extension was opened to coincide with the event. *(MMC)*

10 – Inter-Urban Express Bus Services

While Stockport's transport department was busy building up its bus services within the Borough, and improving its tramway rolling stock, up the road the big neighbour was uneasy.

By the end of 1926, Henry Mattinson, the General Manager of Manchester Corporation Tramways Department, was worried about the effect which the growing number of private bus operators could have on tramway systems by operating buses in parallel with the trams. He decided that if there was a market for fast inter-urban bus services these should be operated by the municipalities.

Accordingly, Manchester commenced a series of cross city services in 1927, and this aroused the interest of other municipal operators in the surrounding area and several sought powers to operate bus services beyond their boundaries.

In August 1927 Oldham Tramways Committee, encouraged by Manchester, called a conference of Transport Managers to discuss the situation and plan the way ahead. This was attended by Manchester, Salford, Oldham, Rochdale, Bury, Bolton, Ashton under Lyne, Stockport and the Stalybridge, Hyde, Mossley and Dukinfield Joint Transport and Electricity Board (SHMD Board). On 2nd September 1927 it was announced that those present had expressed interest in operating through services between Manchester and the various towns represented. One of the principles was to be that there would be operation across Manchester and no termination in the City Centre.

Stockport's initial involvement was in a service from Stockport Dialstone Lane to Bury, via Levenshulme, Piccadilly and Whitefield. It was intended to commence on 28th November 1927 but did not start until 19th December 1927. The service was jointly operated by Stockport, Manchester and Bury and for a time, the Bury buses operated through to Burnley. There was further development in 1929 when, on 7th January, a service commenced from Stockport to Hollinwood. On 15th May 1929 a service from Stockport to Manchester Victoria Street commenced, which was in effect a short working on the Bury route and operating between the Bury times, gave a 15min frequency between Stockport and Manchester. This service was extended as from 25th November 1929, to Monton and Worsley (after the independent Tognarelli had been bought out). Both these services were jointly operated by Stockport and Manchester. There were two additions to the express services in 1930, both involving extensions of Manchester to Reddish services. On 19th October 1930 there was an extension to Andrew Square, Stockport and on 29th October 1930 a further extension to Vernon Park, Stockport, jointly operated by Stockport and Manchester.

As the express services became established there were echoes of the horse tram days three decades earlier as they gave rise to complaints from the police regarding congestion, particularly

Form an orderly queue please – passengers prepare to board Sharps AEC Q for the journey to Winton (beyond Eccles and Monton) in the posed shot at Victoria Bridge, Manchester. The canopy of a Salford bus can be seen on the bridge itself whilst in the left background stand the impressive Victoria Buildings which were destroyed in the blitz. Thomas Cook's office here booked tickets for trips on the River Irwell, below and to the right. The bus – AMV 124, bodied by Weymanns – had been a demonstrator for a year before Sharps purchased it. *(BCVM AEL 2128a)*

in Market Street, Manchester, and its Chief Constable in 1931 insisted that the express bus services be kept away from Market Street and that they did not wait in the City Centre. There were also objections from the taxi owners regarding congestion and from the railways who claimed to be losing revenue to the express bus services.

In order to address these complaints, many of the services were split in Manchester City Centre, in some cases involving a journey between the terminus of the southern section and the terminus of the northern section, much as can be the case in 2008 between the Shudehill interchange and Chorlton Street and Piccadilly. The Bury service was split on 25th October 1931, the two halves becoming the 20 and 35 services. On 8th November 1931 the Vernon Park express service

The Leyland Tiger TS3 had a six-cylinder petrol engine and was ideal for fast long-distance work, even if the speed limits of the day were way below its capability. It had a drop-frame chassis which allowed the body to sit lower, and to create much more attractive designs. Number 159, JA 1465, was the first of the six purchased by Stockport in 1930. *(BCVM 8999/9000a)*

was diverted to operate from the new bus station in Manchester Piccadilly, then known as Parker Street. A Manchester to Poynton express service was started on 15th February 1932 operated jointly by Manchester, Stockport and North Western in competition with the service operated by Sharps to Woodford. The Worsley express service was split on 20th March 1933 and on 9th April the Vernon Park express service was extended to Romiley.

Description of New Omnibus Depôt.

THE New 'Bus Depot, in Heaton Lane, is erected on land forming the site of Wilkinson's Mill and a portion of the Old Gas Works.

Operations were commenced on January 26th, 1931, in pulling down the old buildings and clearing the site. The whole of the old bricks have been utilised to fill up the basements of the Mill and other voids on the Gas Works site, by hand packing and levelling up to form a solid foundation for the floor of the new Shed.

The Transport Department's new bus depot, adjoining the offices and tram sheds at Heaton Lane, created a very substantial and well-designed complex which was in use until the end of the Stockport system's separate existence. It was eventually replaced by the modern Daw Bank facility, further towards the railway viaduct in this view, after the formation of SELNEC in 1969. That then became the headquarters for SELNEC's Southern Division. *(GMTS both)*

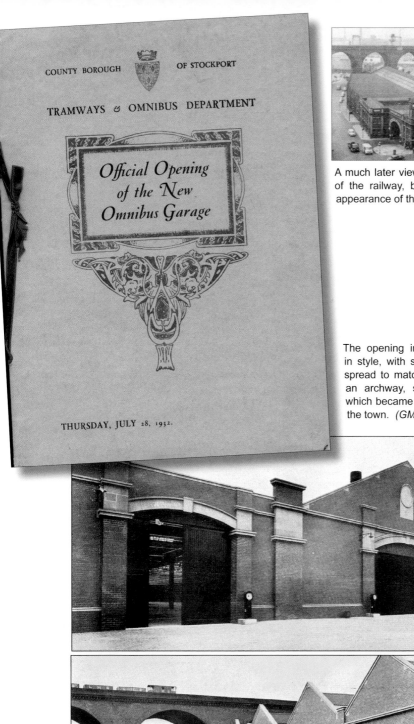

County Borough of Stockport

Tramways & Omnibus Department

Official Opening of the New Omnibus Garage

Thursday, July 28, 1932.

A much later view, after the electrification of the railway, but showing the general appearance of the complex. *(NDC)*

The opening in 1932 was carried out in style, with suitable ceremony and a spread to match. Access was through an archway, surmounted by a clock which became another fine landmark in the town. *(GMTS)*

11 – Greater Emphasis on the Buses Now

The growth of the bus fleet has been noted and as part of the reorganisation after the Gatley tram section was abandoned, a new bus service to Gatley commenced on 28th December 1930, and also two services to Adswood began operating, one via Shaw Heath and the other via Edgeley, this latter service being short lived and ceasing to operate in February 1931. A service to Woodbank, Hempshaw Lane and Cheadle Heath commenced on 13th June 1932 and the service to Woodsmoor was extended in February 1933. On 20th April 1933 the Lowndes Lane service commenced and certain journeys on the Romiley express service were extended to Greave with effect from 17th May 1934.

For an urban area, Stockport was late in its initial operation of double-deck buses although in 1930 as we have seen an AEC Regent with Short Brothers body was tested on loan, but considered unsuitable owing to the number of overhanging trees in what was still quite a rural area – it was returned in September that year.

It was therefore not until 1934 that the Corporation purchased its first double-deckers, these being two Leyland TD3 models with Leyland metal-framed bodies numbered 165 & 166, and they were employed on the Stockport - Cheadle - Gatley service. As a result of this late entry into double-deck operation Stockport was unusual, among regular purchasers of Leyland buses, in not operating that doyen of Leyland bodies of the late 'twenties and early 'thirties generally described as the 'piano fronted body' due to the design of the front of the upper saloon.

Whilst this milestone was being reached for the buses all was not lost for the trams, however, for a new tram service was introduced from Reddish to Hazel Grove on 15th April 1935 operating over existing tracks. That year also saw the celebrations to commemorate the Silver Jubilee of King George V's reign and, as usual, a tram was duly decorated and illuminated ready to tour the system. Balcony car 27 was selected for the job and two years later it would again be decorated, but this time for the Coronation of King George VI following the death of his father and the abdication of his brother. After that it was returned to a quiet corner of the depot where it was left to reflect on its moments of glory.

Meanwhile the process of eliminating the competition continued and on 6th August 1936 Stockport, Manchester Corporation Transport

and North Western concluded negotiations with independent operator Sharps to take over its Woodford route and co-ordinated it with the Poynton service. The cost was £10,500.

From this time onwards, double-deckers featured regularly in Stockport's orders for new buses and up to and including 1940, all were of Leyland manufacture with Leyland bodies. Those supplied in 1935, 1936 and 1937 were of the TD4c variety, the 'c' signifying that they were fitted with torque convertors rather than a conventional clutch and gearbox. This system was introduced by Leyland partly in an attempt to simplify the driving for ex-tram drivers by eliminating the need for the driver to be involved with gear changing. Buses so fitted, normally carried the words 'GEARLESS BUS' on the radiator and became a familiar sight as the system appealed to municipal operators faced with increasing traffic levels and the need to train tram drivers to drive buses as tram replacement schemes were planned. This system was much less efficient than conventional transmission systems.

As a result of this, many operators replaced the torque convertor system with conventional clutch and gearbox and Stockport modified all its vehicles in this way between 1945 and 1947 and may have modified its existing vehicles earlier had it not been for the war. It has been reported that another downside of this transmission allowed a number of minor accidents to occur due to drivers failing to ensure that the vehicle was out of gear and that the handbrake was fully on, thus allowing the bus to creep forward.

In 1936 the long serving General Manager Mr AT Eardley retired and the short list for his replacement contained a number of names which were or were to become well known in the industry. They included R Smith Asher, General Manager of York Corporation Tramways and Omnibuses, Albert F Neal, then Deputy GM at Edinburgh but later to become General Manager of Manchester Corporation Transport, and Cyril Frank Wolsey, General Manager of Douglas Corporation Transport who had been Traffic Manager under Mr Eardley between 1930 and 1932. The successful candidate was Mr C Warwick Wroth, previously Chief Engineer of North Western Road Car.

Mr Wroth applied his engineering expertise both to the buses and the tramway, and amongst other things achieved during his tenure was the installation of a Forest City Electric Co Ltd automatic electric point turner at Wellington Road/Princes Street junction.

Stockport's first double-deckers, Leyland Titan TD3s numbers 165/6, had the distinctive V-fronted Leyland metal-framed bodywork seen opposite and alongside which proved to be something of a disaster for its manufacturer, but these two examples lasted for 24 years before withdrawal. The first of the pair, number 165 is seen at Leyland when new, ready for delivery down the A6. Comparison with the Tiger TS3 on page 55 will reveal that the Borough's Coat of Arms has now been changed for the later version. *(BCVM L5163/4a)*

Facing Page: Number 167, the first of the four TD3c models delivered in 1935, was photographed in Cheadle on the Gatley service for which they had been purchased.

Above: Number 169, JA 6215, from the same batch at Leyland before delivery to Stockport. The large rectangular emergency window at the rear of the upper deck was replaced on the succeeding model by a distinctively-shaped one as seen on page 62. *(BCVM L7831a, 6322a)*

Leyland torque-convertor vehicles carried the wording ***Gearless Bus*** on the radiator front grille as can be seen opposite, also on the sliding driver's window above the engine. Another, more obvious, give-away was the combined double-tank arrangement – below right – which replaced the conventional Autovac fuel pump (manufactured in Stockport) as seen below left. By chance a brass filler cap survived in the pits after the conversions to conventional clutch and gearbox, as seen far left. *(BCVM 5163a, 7875a, below; JAS courtesy PPC, far left)*

When the 1936 delivery of Leyland Titans came they were birds of a very different feather. Numbered 171-8 they were of the TD4c torque-convertor model, but this batch had the new Colin Bailey-designed body which was to be instantly recognisable until Leyland stopped bus body production in 1954. Bailey had been recruited to sort out the problems Leyland had been experiencing following the changeover from wooden-framed bodywork to metal, of which the V-fronted TD3 had been the first example. A major design rework followed, and many operators returned their earlier TD3s to Leyland for major remedial work. We have found no record of Stockport doing this and they were able to obtain 24 years from their examples – certainly not a problem! Here we see three splendid views of Stockport 173, JA 7573, at Leyland before delivery. *(BCVM 7992a, 7995a, 7993a)*

Mr Wroth also introduced Estler trolley heads to replace the former swivel type on the trams, thereby greatly increasing route availability. On the bus side he was responsible for the purchase of 20 of the very distinctive single-decker Leylands, Tiger TS7/8s with centre-entrance bodywork from English Electric, supplier of many of the fleet's tramcars. They carried numbers 183-202 and one has been fully restored to working order to join the ranks of preserved Stockport vehicles.

It appears, however, that he may have had some difficulty in his dealings with his former boss at NWRC, a man he had worked with from the very beginnings of that Company, and at one stage George Cardwell, NWRC's Chairman was called in to act as mediator between Wroth, fighting his corner for the Corporation, and Womar, standing his ground for BET. Whatever the actual details Wroth resigned in 1938, taking a position with Trinidad Leaseholds (a BET subsidiary) before later becoming General Manager of Potteries Motor Traction where he remained until 1958.

Mr Wroth's resignation must have come as something of a surprise after such a short time in office, and Chief Clerk FN Barlow was made Acting Manager until the appointment of the GM's successor was finalised.

The vacancy was filled by the appointment of Mr Eric Booth Baxter as General Manager. He had already had a long career in the passenger transport industry, commencing as a junior with Blackpool Corporation Transport in 1913.

Captions facing: The final frontage of the tram depot, together with the office block, as seen from Mersey Square. This view was taken around 1936/7.

The lower view shows a sylvan scene in St Peter's Square, around the same time, with tram 85 and newly-delivered Leyland TD4c number 173 waiting for their next journeys to Manchester Exchange and Gatley respectively. *(MMC; PA)*

Below: English Electric took this view of number 184, JA 7584, before delivery but, unlike the view at the foot of the page, the use of a different photographic emulsion has lost the difference between the shade of red and the maroon flash. *(RMC)*

English Electric presented Mr Wroth with a framed portrait of one of the 20 centre-entrance single-deckers and it hung in the Manager's Office at Mersey Square for many years. During the demolition of that complex it was found in a pool of water at the bottom of a pit and after much *tlc* shows us (almost!) what these vehicles were like in their prime. Their long lives ensures we shall see them again later in this book. *(JAS courtesy Cliff Marsh)*

The Plaza cinema, opened in October 1932, dominated the south side of the square and the adjacent steps provided the perfect viewpoint for bus and tram spotters alike. Afternoon tea in the cinema's cafe was an optional extra! *(STA)*

The view across Mersey Square continued to appeal to publishers of picture postcards, happily for transport historians, and these two views show the appearance after the next phase of covering the river between the two bridges had been accomplished in 1936. One of the Corporation's Tiger TS8 single-deckers is prominent in the foreground whilst just visible to its left is a North Western single-decker, standing by the offices used by that company.

The two tram tracks under the bus will become the interlaced line below Wellington Road bridge on the line to Cheadle.

Another bus speeds behind the two unsuspecting ladies, passing the transport offices, and the fire station stands, imposing as ever, beyond that. In the centre of the picture a tram stands at the loading island and others can be seen in the distance on Wellington Road. The recently built Heaton Lane clock tower stands out well. *(STA both)*

67

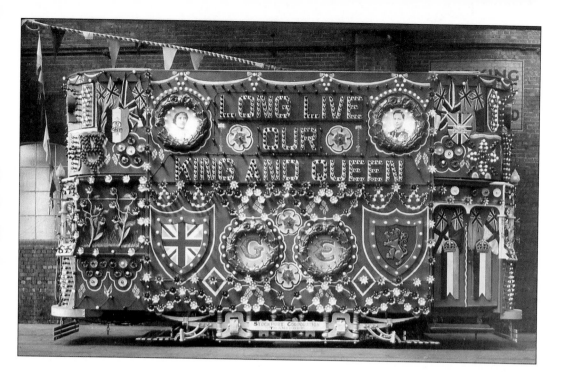

Decorating trams, and later, buses, was quite an art, possibly inspired or encouraged by Blackpool's famous illuminations. Royal occasions were always hot favourites and these two pages give a flavour of some of the spectacles seen on Stockport's streets over the years. Facing page top left is car 27 decorated to mark the Silver Jubilee of King George V and Queen Mary in 1935 This page, above, shows car 27 again, now decorated in 1937 for Coronation of King George VI. When a bus was decorated in this manner it needed to be filled with batteries to provide sufficient power, and so a life-expired vehicle was usually chosen. Number 133, a Cravens-bodied Leyland Lion, was decorated for the Silver Jubilee, and again for the 1937 Coronation as shown below. *(MMC all)*

Car 45 looks spruce and tidy as it was caught operating on the main line to Manchester in the mid-'thirties. Originally built in 1906 it was totally enclosed in 1933 as seen here. Note the multitude of small windows on the lower vestibule to clear the swinging arm of the car's handbrake. *(NDC)*

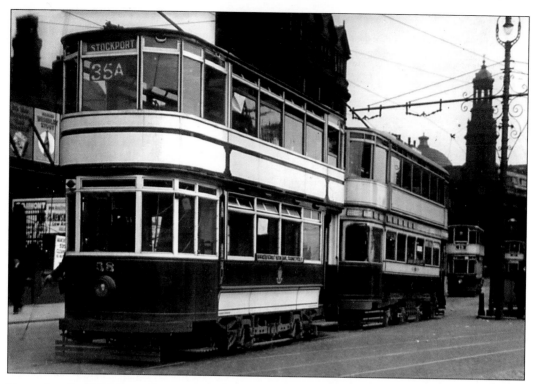

The run from the Rising Sun at Hazel Grove to Manchester took some 59 minutes. In the view above car 58 awaits its turn to use the crossover in Victoria Street before heading back towards Market Street and home. Out of sight to the right are the Victoria buildings which were totally destroyed in the blitz, forcing a temporary move of terminus from here to High Street as seen later. Another prewar view and other landmark which disappeared after the blitz was this triangular complex in George Street, Piccadilly which formed the terminus for car 77. Rylands building is still immediately recognisable today on the corner of Tib Street. Manchester's car 151 looks somewhat down at heel reflecting Manager RS Pilcher's advancing replacement plans for his tramway system. *(MMC both)*

In 1921 Mr Baxter became Traffic Manager at Blackpool. From there he moved on to South Shields, Maidstone and Bournemouth before being appointed Traffic Superintendent at Bradford Corporation Transport in 1935, a position which he retained until his appointment at Stockport. Relations with North Western were said to have improved after his arrival, and he remained as General Manager until his retirement in 1962.

Before Mr Wroth left in 1938 he had also been busy initiating another rebuilding programme for the vestibuling of the remaining open platform cars, some of which still retained the reversed staircases from the beginning of the system. The transport union secretary could finally consider this little matter, pending from 1916, about to be closed! It had also been considered sensible to acquire some good-quality second-hand rail which was now on offer following the closure of the Preston system in December 1934, and also from Manchester following the lifting of the tracks in Middleton Road.

In an interesting aside it is recorded that Stockport had difficulty cutting the Middleton Road rail they had just purchased and sought advice from Manchester as to the reason. All was revealed when the latter's permanent way engineer then pointed out that the rails had been hardened to counteract the effect of track braking!

In deference to its advancing years the 1915 Dennis tower wagon was joined by a more modern brother in 1938, this one apparently replacing an AEC which it may be assumed was a conversion of one of the original buses. Costing £700 and registered ADB 553 it was works fleet No. 105.

During 1938/9 a significant revision was made to the livery when the tramcar's upper-deck panels were painted red, bringing them into line with the buses. Initially the rocker panels were also similarly treated but they were shortly returned to white, as previously. Very soon there would be another livery modification as the bus roofs were painted dark grey to make them less conspicuous to the Luftwaffe.

Also in 1939, orders were placed for six more double-decker buses, three from Leyland and three from Crossley, these being the first double-deckers ordered by Stockport from Crossley. In the event only two Crossleys were delivered due to wartime restrictions and the first of these No. 203 was featured in 'The Transport World' dated

New and old liveries, also the double letter 'H' on the dash of the lowbridge car for the Hyde route. (MMC)

Old and new tower wagons, with ADB 553 standing respectfully in the distance. *(MMC)*

10th April 1941. The Crossley bodies were built on steel framework supplied by Metropolitan Cammell Weymann Limited. As mentioned later, the third Crossley arrived in 1946 as Stockport's first postwar bus. The fleet numbering arrangement for these vehicles was unusual in that the Leylands were allocated even numbers 202, 204, 206 (see opposite) and the Crossleys odd numbers 203, 205 and 207.

In 1939, just before the arrival of the Leyland TD7s below, the tramcar livery for the totally enclosed cars was modified to bring it in line with the buses, but there was later a small modification to the rocker panels (below the waist where the crest can be seen) which reverted to white. The route board is seen below. *(MMC; JAS; STA)*

BORO BOUNDARY (CHEADLE) STOCKPORT, REDDISH

Manchester's Albert Square, terminus of the 35C, and car 6 stands with the Corporation's buses. The new Leyland double-decker is on the Limited Stop service to Gatley where once Stockport's trams terminated, of course. Tram number 6 was an entirely home-made production by Stockport, assembled from spare parts and completed by bespoke bits to fill the gaps, and fitted to a truck which was also spare. Waste not want not – it was this policy of re-utilisation of assets which made the Department so efficient. *(MMC)*

Although we have seen that Stockport was still investing in its tramway, and was acquiring materials such as rail when they became available at advantageous rates, there had been a decision in January 1936 to abandon the Edgeley route. Fortunately, as events turned out, this decision was rescinded twelve months later, and Stockport would survive to be the last tramcar operator in the Manchester conurbation.

Stuart Pilcher, Manchester's General Manager, had proposed the abandonment of that city's trams by 1939/40 and had it not been for the outbreak of war in that year he might have achieved his aim. Shortages of petrol and rubber, and the inability to take normal deliveries of new buses, thwarted any attempts at wholesale replacement of trams until after 1946 – unless there were exceptional circumstances. Stockport was less eager to dispense with an asset which still paid its way and provided an extremely efficient service to its citizens – scope for differences in the post-war years as we shall see later.

One of Manchester's impressive bogie cars stands in Mersey Square, the differing gradients being quite marked from this viewpoint. The Corporation was not willing to allow these cars to operate up Daw Bank to St Peter's Square and so this was their terminus in the town centre. Stockport 58 displays the route number 3 and destination Reddish for the number 3 service. In the view below at Hazel Grove the two leading cars display the tell-tale sign of too close depot parking where the headlamp rims have caught on the next car, usually because of uneven heights of collision fenders. One slight nudge was sufficient to badly dent the dash. *(MMC both)*

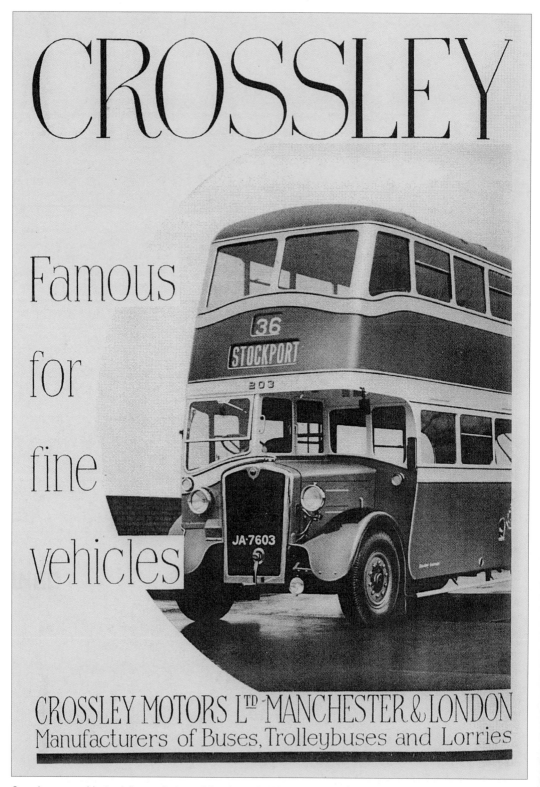

CROSSLEY

Famous for fine vehicles

36
STOCKPORT
203

JA·7603

CROSSLEY MOTORS L^{TD} MANCHESTER & LONDON
Manufacturers of Buses, Trolleybuses and Lorries

Crossley were able to deliver only two of the three double-deckers Stockport had ordered before they had to devote all their efforts to war work. The body design is very similar to the Manchester streamline standard apart from destination layout and other small details. *(STA)*

12 – Wartime

With the outbreak of war in 1939, and the consequent shortages of petrol, diesel and rubber (to take just three prime examples), the trams became an even more valuable asset. There were still 83 cars in the fleet though not all were fit for passenger service, some having been used as works cars for a number of years. No cars were lost to enemy action but number 14 was withdrawn following a collision in 1944.

Neighbouring Manchester had been gradually reducing its tramway network and rolling stock after the arrival of R Stuart Pilcher as Manager in 1929, and formally agreed in 1937 to abandon the rest of its tramway, but this conversion had to be postponed because of the war; Stockport had fortunately quickly rescinded a 1936 decision to scrap the Edgeley route, and thus was still running its network as it had been from 1931 after the Gatley section was abandoned.

The town was surrounded by manufacturers whose commitment to the war effort would require greatly increased public transport provision, and at all times of the day and night, with day-working and shift-working often meaning they were working round the clock. With organisations including Avro, Hans Renold, Mirrlees, Crossley, Davies & Metcalfe, Beyer, Peacock, and Gorton Railway Works requiring transport for their workers, Stockport's buses and trams were going to be busy. Comparing like-for-like, whereas 12million passengers had been carried on the trams in 1914, in 1943 the figure would reach an all-time high of over 32.8million. With the arrival of the five buses in 1940 the bus fleet stood at 93.

It was realised that in this war, the great danger would be from aerial attack, and that blackout restrictions would need to be imposed as a matter of urgency. Local mills would have been busy producing the necessary blackout material for homes and other buildings throughout the land, ready to hang in windows and supplement curtains to ensure no light escaped to guide the German planes to their targets. The Department's buses were quickly given a coat of dark grey paint over the white roof areas – basically in line with the

A carefully posed shot records the arrival of this wartime delivery, Crossley number 203 in 1940, just in time to use the newly-opened Mersey Way which covered the river as can be seen. The tram on the left has just departed from Mersey Square and is passing the Transport Offices; Daw Bank, also known as Undercliff, leading up to St Peter's Square, is just out of view to the right. Almost unbelievably, the whole of this area would later disappear under the Mersey Way Shopping Precinct in the 1960s. *(MMC)*

trams – and North Western, Manchester and all operators were similarly occupied. Government restrictions on the amount of light which could be emitted were draconian, and headlamp masks were fitted to all vehicles, as can be seen in our photographs. Petrol rationing meant that private motoring for pleasure was a thing of the past and the roads became deserted apart from military and public transport vehicles. Men were called up to serve in the armed forces and in April 1941 conductresses once again returned to the fray – 190 were employed by 1944.

The town's first air raid warning was heard in August 1940, whilst in October that year a new Traffic Superintendent (TS) joined the Department. Mr G Beckett came from Oldham, where he had been Chief Inspector. The new TS was given a true baptism of fire, for the following day air raids caused chaos with major damage in Princes Street and Hillgate.

This was only a foretaste of worse to come. At Christmas time 1940 there was a huge air raid on Manchester, with incendiary bombs destroying many warehouses and offices in the city centre and creating fires whose flames could be seen as far away as Bolton, and lighting the night sky with an awesome orange glow which guided the planes back on successive nights before all the fires could be extinguished. Stockport was fortunate to escape that measure of destruction, though many of these fire bombs did fall in the town and Heaton Lane depot was hit. The enormous damage inflicted in Piccadilly and on the Victoria Buildings at the foot of Market Street in Manchester meant that the tram services to Exchange had to be cut back to High Street, whilst the George Street terminus of the 35z was gutted by fire.

After all the efforts to safeguard the trams using the two lowbridges, the unthinkable happened in

High Street, Manchester – the temporary terminus for cars unable to access Victoria Street after the 1940 blitz. The clear up operation took some months and the prominent Victoria Buildings had been completely gutted by fire. In this view the cars are facing Lewis's building, and will turn to their left to enter Market Street. Modern Metrolink trams do just that, and also had a station platform here for some time. *(MMC)*

January 1941 when car 39 became jammed under the Bredbury bridge, badly damaging its top cover. There were still sufficient skilled workers in the Department to be able to cope with such emergencies, and the top cover was recovered from car 27, long out of service after having been decorated for the Coronation. Such was the need for trams that two open top cars which had survived as works cars were – as meagre resources allowed – top-covered and returned to service in 1944 as passenger cars, including the original number 1 which had for many years been the home of the Department's upholsterer in Mersey Square depot.

Once again scrap metal became a vital commodity and very soon iron railings were commandeered to be melted down for the greater need. Aluminium pans were also sought at one stage, supposedly for aircraft production, though it was later claimed that this may have been more of a morale-boosting exercise.

The emergency lamp above the masked headlamp can be seen on car 25, with the edge of the original numeral showing beneath it. The smaller numerals were normally applied to buses. Note also the large letter H either side of the headlamp, indicating a low height car which could pass beneath the two railway bridges. *(MMC)*

In January 1942 a visit was made to Hull to inspect and consider the purchase of 12 trams, by then surplus to requirements in that town. After due consideration it was decided to take no action and the cars in question were soon purchased by Leeds, together with a further 20 from the same town later that year.

A collision in the blackout in 1943 next focused the Department's electrical engineer Maurice Marshall's mind on another problem. A stationary Manchester car, showing no lights because of a dewirement, was run into by the following Stockport car whose driver was unable to see the unlit mass in front of him. Mr Marshall produced a battery-powered emergency red light which was activated by a relay when the traction power failed or was cut off. These lamps were quickly fitted to all Stockport's trams, above the headlamp, where they obscured the fleet numbers. New numbers were applied, using the smaller numerals normally applied to buses. Careful scrutiny of the illustrations in the book will reveal this, and any tram carrying such a lamp must have been photographed post-1943.

A long-standing link with the past was severed with the retirement in February 1943 of Rolling Stock Superintendent Herbert Wood, a man who had joined the Department in 1904. Another link with the past was recorded when former Manager ET Eardley died in that same year, the year that the trams carried their highest number of passengers ever – 32.8million, with 2.2million car miles being operated. Princes Street tracks were relaid in May, reflecting the intense use and the damage inflicted by the air raid in 1940. Lancashire Hill was the next candidate for relaying and the down line was replaced between August and October. If rail purchased from Manchester was being used for this work the ex-Middleton Road material which had proved so difficult to cut would have been ideal for Lancashire Hill, having been hardened

to resist the effects of track brakes which were clearly the reason that only the down line needed replacing here.

It was in that year that Stockport obtained its first new buses since the five which had been delivered in 1940. A handful of vehicles were withdrawn, being completely worn out, and some were 'traded in' against Government permits for new Utility buses on a one-for-one basis.

During wartime, those operators who were able to justify new vehicles had no choice with regard to manufacturers, standardisation went out of the window, and vehicles were allocated by the Ministry of War Transport. In view of this, many operators who received new vehicles received more than one make of chassis and often several makes of body. Stockport was unusual (and quite fortunate) in that its entire wartime allocation comprised 16 Guy Arab 2 chassis all fitted with bodies built by Massey Brothers of Wigan. The bodies were built to the standard specification

Hardly elegant perhaps, but there is truth in the old adage that handsome is as handsome does, and these utility Guys gave almost as many years service as most operators would expect from a peacetime model. Piccadilly is the familiar location and the bus is bound for Dialstone Lane, Stockport. *(NDC)*

Reliance number 138, seen above in wartime garb, was one of the vehicles which were relinquished in 1941 to allow two new Guy Arab utilities to be allocated to the Department. Almost half of these veterans would have been withdrawn by this time so there were probably no great sighs of dismay to see their departure. *(RM)*

This group of evacuees has just arrived at Tiviot Dale railway station and a selection of buses is ready and waiting to take them to their new, temporary, homes. Everyone looks happy, but a V2 rocket will bring back the horrors all too soon. JA 7577, number 177, is one of the 1936 delivery of TD4c models. *(PPC)*

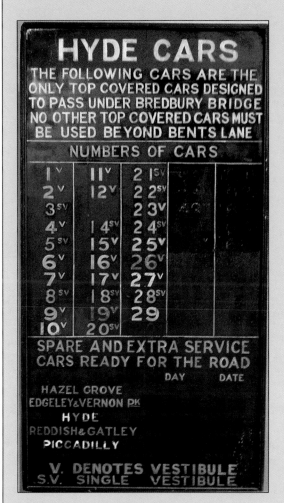

HYDE CARS

THE FOLLOWING CARS ARE THE ONLY TOP COVERED CARS DESIGNED TO PASS UNDER BREDBURY BRIDGE NO OTHER TOP COVERED CARS MUST BE USED BEYOND BENTS LANE

NUMBERS OF CARS

1^V	11^V	21^{SV}	
2^V	12^V	22^{SV}	
3^{SV}		23^V	
4^V	14^{SV}	24^{SV}	
5^{SV}	15^V	25^V	
6^V	16^V	26^V	
7^V	17^V	27^V	
8^{SV}	18^{SV}	28^{SV}	
9^V	19^V	29	
10^V	20^{SV}		

SPARE AND EXTRA SERVICE CARS READY FOR THE ROAD

DAY   DATE

HAZEL GROVE
EDGELEY & VERNON P^K
HYDE
REDDISH & GATLEY
PICCADILLY

V. DENOTES VESTIBULE
S.V. SINGLE VESTIBULE

In 1943 it was decided to renumber the lowbridge cars to bring them into one numerical sequence. This board was duly amended to make sure all concerned were in no doubt as to which were the trams in question. It survives to this day in the Heaton Park Tram Museum in Manchester, one of the many reminders of the region's tramway history which also include a selection of street name signs and ornamental pole bases such as the one below. *(JAS)*

82

which had been produced by the National Federation of Vehicle Trades and Operators Joint Technical and Advisory Committee working in conjunction with the Ministry of Supply and the Ministry of War Transport. They were delivered in grey livery and with a single aperture destination facility at the front, this being a feature of the standard specification. At least some of them are known to have been delivered with slatted wooden seating.

The Guy Arab chassis was noted for its rugged simplicity with the result that operators had many years of service from these chassis, some of which were rebodied in the postwar period. The same could not be said of wartime bodies, with the exception of the metal-framed variety manufactured by Northern Counties Motor and Engineering Company of Wigan and by East Lancashire Coachbuilders of Blackburn. Bodies which were not replaced in the postwar period often underwent extensive rebuilding. Stockport, however, managed to get 18-20 years service out of the Massey bodies without any evidence of the extensive rebuilding which had taken place on wartime bodies in many other fleets. Perhaps this speaks volumes for the maintenance team at Stockport. During the postwar period some of the Guys had their wooden seating replaced by upholstered seating and all had service number apertures added alongside the destination aperture at the front.

Although the Guys were delivered in a grey livery, Stockport retained its standard livery for the other vehicles in the fleet during the wartime period, save for the grey roofs already mentioned. This may have resulted from Stockport having good stocks of paint in the stores. The Guy Arab was available with both the 5LW and 6LW Gardner engine but all the Stockport examples had the smaller 5LW engine. The earlier Guy Arab 1 had an extended bonnet when fitted with the 6LW engine but all Arab 2 models had the extended bonnet regardless of the engine fitted.

Opposite page foot: A rare and fascinating if technically poor wartime shot in Mersey Square showing, right to left, two of Stockport's centre-entrance Tigers with English Electric bodywork, a Daimler with Northern Counties bodywork from the SHMD fleet, and an unidentified North Western single-decker which could be a Bristol, a Dennis or a Tilling-Stevens with Eastern Counties or ECW bodywork. *(PPC)*

Somewhat belatedly it was decided to renumber the lowbridge trams into one sequence – 1-30 – in an attempt to prevent another Bredbury Bridge incident and this led to another renumbering exercise when the highbridge open balcony cars were renumbered in the sequence 31-45. All this activity must have kept someone in the paintshop busy for a little while.

The heavy increase in traffic was now causing great concern to the Department, especially on part of the main tram line to Manchester where track laid by Manchester in 1923 was now completely worn out, and an order was given by the Transport Committee that cars must not exceed half speed on the worst part of that line. Wartime restrictions meant that permission had to be obtained for such major renewals and Stockport was obliged to get a Ministry inspection in April 1944 before it won the approval to apply for the necessary steel allocation for track replacement. Work finally began in February 1945 and was not without its difficulties. Manchester Corporation became involved using its Direct Labour department and numbers of German PoWs were employed on the project which was not completed until July 1946. The work involved the stretch between Crossley Road and Belmont Bridge and one track at a time was relaid using single-line working to maintain a service.

The need for scrap metal continued long after the war was over – this advertisement was placed in Transport World in May 1948. *(STA)*

Wartime Mersey Square, with two views of PLSC Lion number 124, the Cravens body recognisable by its shallow windows, and Guy Utility 216 in wartime garb but with matt paint on the roof contrasting with the sheen of the body panels. Note that both vehicles display the garter logo on the rear panels whilst the Lion also has two white warning patches. *(Maurice Marshall collection courtesy Chris Heaps)*

In May 1944, Chief Inspector Bowlas retired. Like former Rolling Stock Engineer Wood he had joined the undertaking as far back as 1904 and for many years had recorded events and people connected with Stockport's transport, his camera and tripod being familiar appendages to one and all. Some of his work is known to be included in the Maurice Marshall collection used in this book but, unfortunately, is not individually identifiable.

In July a further eight Guy Arabs arrived, bringing the bus fleet to 97 and they were quickly put to use moving a large influx of evacuees moved into the town from bombed areas. These people's peace of mind would not have been eased by the unwanted appearance of a V2 flying bomb shortly afterwards!

The arrival of 1945, with hopes that end of the war could not be far away now, also brought fresh concerns about the state of the SHMD trams which were becoming unsafe. Ministry approval to withdraw them was obtained and they were withdrawn from the Stockport-Hyde service from 19th May, with a ceremonial last car running through Hyde town centre on 29th May. The Green Linnets would be heard no more.

The war had now finished and the illuminated tram was suitably decorated, and toured the system for four successive nights. It was then scrapped – clearly there was going to be nothing else worth celebrating after that!

Six more Utility Guys arrived next, the final deliveries of these vehicles, bringing the bus fleet to 103 whilst the tram fleet now stood at 81 specimens of assorted shapes, sizes, ages and usefulness.

Just exactly what would happen next must have taxed everyone. Huge amounts of bomb damage, worn-out public transport, men still away in the forces, enormous debts to pay for the war, forthcoming elections and no small measure of unrest as there had been after the end of the First War.

There were going to be challenging times for the Department and the country.

Leyland Tiger 163, JA 1469, looks decidedly down at heel in this post war view on what must have been quite a hot day – note the open windows, of the pull-down type similar to those on the trams, not the wind-down which became more popular. Note also the handle to release the emergency exit behind the driver's door. The bus will have put in good service since it was delivered in 1930 and ran until 1951, when all bar one of the batch of six were withdrawn. Route 39, a short-working of the number 9, ran from Parrs Wood to serve the Renold Chains factory. *(AEJ)*

Just as it was necessary to apply to renew infrastructure, so it was also necessary to get permission to scrap it, including tracks and vehicles. The older SHMD cars were apparently becoming unsafe and decidedly dangerous, and in May 1945 permission was obtained to scrap them all. Here car 63, one of the 1925 build, is seen looking quite presentable on a glorious sunny day but the masked headlamp confirms that this is indeed a wartime view. *(STA)*

13 – Post War Developments

When the war in Europe ended in May 1945 the timetable for tramway replacement in the region was at the top of many north west towns' agendas. As already recorded the SHMD system was the first to go, where lack of spares and maintenance had led to the deterioration of those trams to such an extent that they were unable to operate the joint service between Edgeley and Hyde, and consequently Stockport took over the complete operation from 19th May 1945. Oldham was the next to succumb, on 3rd August 1946, then Bolton and Salford on 29th and 30th March of 1947 respectively.

All these operators required new buses, some to replace trams and others to replace time-expired pre-war vehicles, and, with the exception of SHMD in the period between 1945 and 1948, all the above would be looking to Leyland Motors and Crossleys for the majority of those buses. SHMD was taking Daimlers, and, fortunately, Charles Baroth also went to Daimler for his big order for almost 200 CVG6 models to rebuild the Salford fleet. Manchester was ordering in hundreds from Leyland, Crossley and Daimler.

Some orders had been placed before the war, other 'reserves' had been made during the war, but now was the day of reckoning. There was a Government edict that exports must come first – to help pay the crippling debts incurred in defeating Nazi Germany – and the bus manufacturers were unable to meet demand for some time. The age of the queue was clearly not over yet. The rate of bus deliveries would determine the actual pace of change from trams to buses, but Stockport had not yet decided whether to abandon its trams and its bus orders were, therefore, more modest.

In anticipation of the above events and in preparation for the possible complete closure of the tramway, together with the need to replace time expired buses following restrictions on purchases

One picture which sums up the early postwar scene. A gloomy view at Manchester's Exchange terminus, with car 50 ready to make the long journey back to its home. No other traffic, just one pedestrian, and only one passenger on the tram by the look of it. Fog hides the badly damaged Exchange railway station buildings, though unlike much of the neighbouring area it is at least still standing. The two adjoining stations – Exchange and Victoria – had been an obvious target and the bombs which destroyed the Victoria Buildings behind the photographer and the Baxendale's complex in Shudehill were only a stone's throw from their likely intended targets. *(MMC)*

during the war years, it was time to calculate just how many buses should be ordered.

At this time the bus fleet comprised 39 double-deckers and 44 single-deckers whilst the tram fleet consisted of 81 double-deck trams, the most recent dating from 1926. Consideration thus had to be given to the possible replacement of the trams in addition to the replacement of time expired buses.

At its meeting on 17th December 1945 the Transport Committee agreed to the purchase of 20 double-deck buses, and tenders for these were invited. By the time of the meeting in February 1946, ten tenders had been received, two for complete vehicles, three for chassis and five for bodies. These were to the prewar standard width of 7ft 6ins but by then General Manager EB Baxter had received intimation that the maximum width was soon to be increased to 8ft 0ins. In view of this the Committee resolved to seek new tenders for the supply of wider buses.

A letter was received at this meeting from Crossley Motors Ltd referring to the 1939 order for three buses, of which only two had been delivered. A revised quotation of £2,930 was offered and this was accepted. Stockport's first postwar bus was therefore now on order, and materialised as number 207 carrying registration JA 7607, both numbers as allocated in 1941. It was very different, however, from the Manchester streamline style Mancunians delivered in 1940 as the photographs on the next pages clearly show.

This was thus the start of Stockport's extensive fleet renewal in the years immediately following the end of hostilities in 1945. In that same year Crossley Motors had moved its factory from Gorton, Manchester to Erwood Park just over the Manchester boundary on the outskirts of Stockport and ironically many workers used the Crossley Road and Manchester tram service to go to work to build buses.

In March 1946 the General Manager advised the Committee that difficulties had arisen with regard to the 8ft 0ins wide vehicles which were not yet available, and that insistence on this width would result in delays. It was agreed that such

... and its not much busier here either! The policeman, positioned directly below the overhead lamp, for his safety, waves the Edgeley bound tram into Greek Street, whilst some lucky person has just acquired a Standard Vanguard car. Most cars were going for export at this time and it was quite an event to see a new one – it must be c1947 now. In the background the imposing Town Hall stands majestically on the A6, while the Belisha beacons have not been restored yet – one is still painted black, the other has been decapitated. The lone cyclist dutifully awaits the signal to allow him to proceed. *(MMC)*

delays were not acceptable and the original ten tenders were reconsidered.

Arising from this, visits were made to Crossley Motors and Leyland Motors factories in March and early April 1946, and the decision was made to purchase complete vehicles from Crossley Motors at a price of £2,904 10s 0d. each. The 20 buses were to be numbered 225-44, following on from the wartime Guys 209-24.

In 1946, as mentioned, Oldham's trams were withdrawn, and nearer home the Manchester Exchange to Reddish tramway was replaced by buses although Stockport continued to operate trams at peak periods.

The tram service from Edgeley to Hyde was next cut back to Vernon Park on 2nd March 1947, and a new bus service was established between Mersey Square and Hyde Market Place to replace the trams. On 3rd May 1947 the rush hour trams to Woodley were withdrawn and replaced the following day by a bus service to Bents Lane with extension to Woodley at rush hour. No trams were withdrawn as a result of these revised arrangements, although two which had been involved in collisions were withdrawn in 1947.

By this time the 20 much-needed 7ft 6ins wide Crossley-bodied Crossleys had arrived, allowing more of the Leyland PLSC Lions from 1927/8,

and Reliances from 1929/30 to be disposed of.

However, the postwar expansion in travel was now well under way, and in December 1946 the Transport Committee received a report from the General Manager indicating that there had been an increase in traffic which had necessitated the substitution of double-deckers on some single-deck routes, and that an additional twelve double-deckers were required. Six tenders were received in January 1947, two for complete vehicles, three for chassis and one for bodies. The Crossley tender for twelve complete buses at £3,500 each was stated to be 'the most suitable although not the lowest', and was accepted. The price escalation of just over 20% in nine months is notable. It is minuted that a letter from Crossley was read before the decision was reached which almost certainly contained reference to local employment.

There was a world of difference between the two Crossley Mancunians delivered in 1940 and the postwar DD42 models of which 207 was the precursor, and which latter type would dominate the Stockport bus scene for many years. The view opposite shows the styling of the new body to good advantage and the raised panelling in the rearmost saloon windows covers the framing for the suspended rear platform – a measure introduced to cut down damage in rear-end collisions and so reduce repair times. *(RM both)*

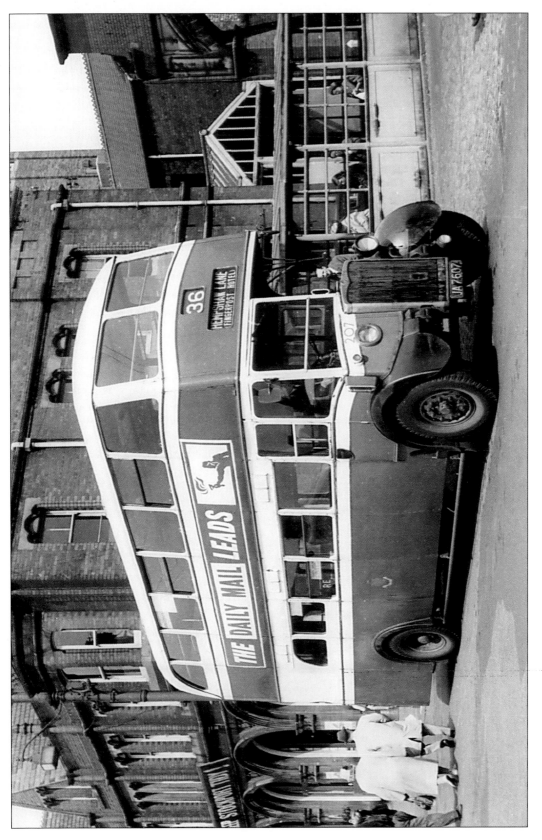

The increase in traffic continued unabated and in April 1947 the order for twelve buses was increased to 20. The buses, still to the then Stockport standard 7ft 6in width, were delivered in 1948, and received fleet numbers 245-64. These new arrangements allowed four of the worst trams to be withdrawn, leaving a mixed bag of some 76 cars still in the fleet.

The end of the tram service to Manchester commenced with the withdrawal of the 35B working between St Peter's Square and Manchester Albert Square, and its replacement by bus service 89 with effect from 16th February 1948. Stockport had normally worked the 35B service on weekdays but the replacement bus service was jointly operated by Stockport and Manchester. Initially the Manchester terminus was Albert Square but in November 1948 this was moved the short distance round the corner to Princes Street, although the destination was still shown as 'Albert Square'.

Plans were made to replace the other tram services 35 and 35C to Manchester, but these were delayed when the Traffic Commissioners refused to grant a licence for the replacement bus service. The reason for this was that North Western had objected on the grounds that it was proposed to operate the service at tram fares which would undercut their own fares. Manchester and Stockport were instructed to revise their fares and submit a revised case, which was then successful. The last full day of tramway operation on service 35 was 9th January 1949 and from the following day bus service 92 commenced operation between Manchester Piccadilly, Stockport and Hazel Grove. The numbers 89 and 92 were part of a series of numbers 89 to 95 reserved by Manchester in 1940 for tramway replacement services.

Service 92 became Stockport's most frequent and most profitable bus route. It was paralleled by two Limited Stop services, service 18 operated between Piccadilly and Stockport, Dialstone Lane but it was later reduced to a Monday to Friday morning and evening peak time service between Manchester Chorlton Street and Stockport, Bramhall Moor Lane. This service had originally been part of the 'Inter-Urban Express Network' when it had operated beyond Manchester to Worsley.

The other Limited Stop service was number 20, which also had its roots in the Inter-Urban express network when it operated from Dialstone Lane to Manchester and on to Bury. When the 92 service commenced it was operating from Piccadilly to Poynton Lostock Road (20) or Woodford (20X) There was therefore a very frequent service along the A6 trunk road from Manchester to Stockport and Hazel Grove as indeed there still is in 2008.

Facing page: An early postwar view inside Mersey Square depot with cars 24, 67, 38 and 8 in view, 67 being raised on jacks to allow the wheelsets to be extracted for attention. Car 24 (still with reversed staircase) sports the small fleet numbers mentioned earlier, the others have had the original style large shaded numerals applied in the lower position. Apart from this change in connection with the emergency lamps little appears to have changed since before the war. *(MMC)*

'The first shall be last . . .' Car 30, above, still retains its reversed staircase, but has been fitted with a six-window top cover produced by the Department. After its reincarnation in 1944 it became the last of the lowbridge cars In the renumbering (1-30) having previously been the original number 1. The sewing machine has now gone!

Brush car 38 in Mersey Square, below, became a highbridge car when it received this UEC top cover in 1907/8 It was never renumbered and lasted almost until the end, being withdrawn in 1950. *(MMC both)*

The wartime Utility deliveries were put into standard livery as soon as resources allowed – and were thereby mightily improved in appearance as can be seen! In the upper view number 209, delivered in 1943 as the first of the Utilities, is sandwiched between a Manchester Corporation double-decker and one of North Western's new single-decker Bristol Ls with its distinctive ECW bodywork, though neither make would be available to NWRC for much longer. If the driver of the Crossley in the lower view is not very careful it will take more than a coat of the newly-advertised Dulux paint to put matters right on 223's rear nearside corner. *(RM both)*

Facing page: Massey bodied Utility Guy Arab number 210, the second to arrive, received a slightly different and more attractive application of the bus livery when it was repainted after the war but, sadly, was the only one so treated. It was standing outside the depot entrance when Roy Marshall recorded it. The extra ivory band was in line with the revised livery by then being applied as the totally enclosed trams were repainted. All the Utilities later received the route number boxes as shown here. *(RM)*

New buses, and the reduction in tram services, allowed withdrawal of more prewar veteran buses. This PLSC Lion, DB 6853, number 113, was one of the last to go when the final ones were withdrawn in 1949. Technically poor, but the only view we have found of a postwar Lion. *(PPC)*

This busy scene in Parker Street bus station shows the revised stand arrangements where the Stockport bound buses are now facing Portland Street, not Mosley Street as in prewar days. Behind number 242 from 1947 stand two prewar ECW-bodied North Western buses, a Dennis saloon and a Bristol double-decker. *(RM)*

Below and facing page: 'Probably one of the UK's best known tramscapes' as Heineken might have put it in their later famous advertisements. *(NDC both)*

A striking picture of a well-known location. Number 241 is about to come a stand at the exit from Hempshaw Lane and the **HALT AT MAJOR ROAD AHEAD** sign can just be seen above the rather unusual finger post pointing to Yorkshire; nearby Derbyshire was perhaps hidden from this angle. CDB 11 was the first of the 1947 delivery of four similar vehicles. Route 36 (Offerton-Finger Post Hotel) terminated at the Finger Post Hotel on the opposite corner from where this photograph was taken. *(NDC)*

The Battersby company was founded in 1868, employing over 1,000 people at its peak. In 1966 it became part of the Association of British Hat Manufacturers. After closure the building became the Museum of Hatting until the contents were transferred to the Hat Factory located in the Wellington Mill and opened in 2000. The Battersby complex now houses a variety of industrial units, and the former loud buzzer for starting and finishing survived for some time.

The 20 Leyland Tigers from 1936/7 with their distinctive English Electric bodies had been a good investment, the first withdrawals not taking place until 1959 after 23 year's service, and the last in 1963 after 26 years. They had been somewhat sidelined from late in 1946 when traffic levels had required double-deckers to take over some of their duties, but could still be seen working rush hour extras on trunk routes such as the 92 late in their lives. Number 192, JA 7592, below, was the last of the batch of TS7s, whilst number 199 above was a TS8. Two of these vehicles were transferred to the Stockport Social Services Department after withdrawal from passenger service and survived into preservation, with JA 7591, formerly 191, now fully restored but retaining its rear wheelchair lift fitted after transfer to Social Services. *(NDC; STA)*

Two trams, one of North Western's Brush-bodied Bristol single-deckers, a Manchester double-decker outside the Transport Offices, a new Crossley double-decker and two English Electric single-deckers – the evocative view from the Plaza cafe in 1947. (CMC)

MERSEY SQUARE, STOCKPORT.

Well, where else would such a bus be making for ? Number 246, neatly posed, was an example of Crossley's model DD42/5 from the 1948 delivery of 20 seen in later life after the fitment of flashing trafficators. Stockport had no 8ft wide Crossleys. *(RGR)*

14 – Decision time for The Trams

The future of Stockport's own tramway now came into focus again when in January 1948 the cost of upkeep of the Reddish tram track was considered, with the question as to whether money should be spent on repairs or whether buses should be substituted. It was agreed that further consideration be given to this, but that in the meantime, tenders should be invited for another 20 double-decker buses.

The tenders for these were received at the March 1948 meeting and totalled twelve, two for chassis or complete vehicles, three for chassis and seven for bodies. How very different from the days when trams were being ordered. Guy and Daimler invited visits to their works and these invitations were accepted, but then the decision was deferred.

By early April 1948 two firms revised their delivery dates but there was still no decision with regard to repair of the tram track. There was then an attempt by the minority party to accept the Crossley tender but this was defeated. In mid-April a further tender was received from an unidentified chassis maker by then able to offer bodies as well as chassis (almost certainly AEC after the tie-up with Park Royal at this time), and a decision was further delayed pending a visit to Leyland Motors in May.

Following this visit, and the clarification of certain items by letter, an order was placed with Leyland Motors for 20 double-deckers at a cost of £72,060. In the meantime a letter had been received from Crossley Motors notifying an error in their tender and requesting a revision.

The tender from Leyland was for PD2/1 models with synchromesh gearboxes, but in September Leyland advised that an earlier delivery date could be achieved if constant mesh gearboxes were substituted in place of the synchromesh type. In his book on 'Postwar Leyland Titans', published by The Transport Publishing Company, Alan Townsin mentions that Leyland had technical problems with this synchromesh gearbox and this could therefore explain matters. In view of the fact that drivers were familiar with constant mesh gearboxes, the revised specification was accepted and Leyland offered a reduction of £30 per vehicle. By October 1949 all the vehicles had been delivered and they were allocated fleet numbers 265-84.

Despite all these smart new buses coming into service the trams remained popular, and with good reason as was apparent at the December 1948 Transport Committee meeting when Mr Baxter reported difficulty with regard to collecting the 1d fares on the Hazel Grove to Crossley Road tram service. The low fares on the trams encouraged high loadings, leaving insufficient time for the collection of fares. How it was resolved was not recorded.

The increased tempo of patronage was continuing and it was agreed to seek tenders for 24 new double-deckers. An identical number of tenders were received, five for chassis, twelve for bodies and seven for complete vehicles. These were discussed on St Valentines Day 1949 but by then the Manchester decision to abandon its trams had been implemented and Stockport's trams were therefore isolated.

The major business of the day therefore centred on whether or not Stockport should follow Manchester and abandon its tramway system. Following discussion it was agreed that, subject to the agreement of the whole council, the remaining trams should indeed be replaced by buses. The die was cast.

Stockport Corporation Transport Department

REVISION OF TRAMCAR SERVICES

HAZEL GROVE and STOCKPORT (St. Peter's Square) No. 4A

MANCHESTER (Piccadilly) and STOCKPORT (St. Peter's Square) No. 35C

On and after Monday, 16th February, 1948, the above named services will be withdrawn from St. Peter's Square, Stockport, and will operate as a through service between Hazel Grove and Manchester (Piccadilly) via the main road.

MANCHESTER (Albert Square) and STOCKPORT (St. Peter's Square) No. 35B

On the same date the above service will be substituted by an Omnibus Service.

Mersey Square,
Stockport.
February.

For details see separate announcement

E. B. BAXTER, A.M. Inst. T.
General Manager.

(STA)

George Street wouldn't seem the same after the departure of the smart red and white four-wheeled Stockport cars (though latterly they had lost their shine), but then neither would the other streets of Manchester after the demise of the city's own trams, one of which is heading down Market Street.

The demolition of the buildings in George Street after they were damaged beyond repair in the blitz allowed Lewis's building to be seen from the Gardens as in the lower view. *(MMC both)*

Facing page: As we like to remember them . . . a pristine Stockport car, recently repainted, would always stand out in Manchester where no trams had been painted since before the war in view of the decision to abandon the system. *(NDC)*

Withdrawal of the 35 service also meant the end of Stockport's trams at the Exchange terminus of course. Here number 76 waits its turn in the queue to reverse and return over the crossover. The Manchester 'Pilcher' in front of number 76 dates the picture quite neatly since all 38 of that class were sold between July 1946 and June 1948, to various operators. *(MMC)*

And finally, it also meant the end of Stockport's trams in Manchester's Albert Square. Here number 60 waits to make its journey home. In the background, behind the monument, the Town Hall extension can be seen. On the right one of Manchester's Titans can be seen at the bus stands which were the focal point for so many homeward journeys over the years. *(MMC)*

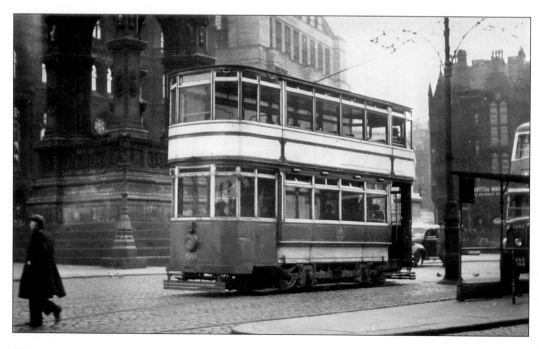

Two contrasting views of Stockport – above, a splendid panorama from the fire station tower showing amongst other recognisable places Mersey Square, Heaton Lane depot, Daw Bank and the railway viaduct, with the A6 cutting across the centre, left to Hazel Grove and right to Manchester. *(NDC)*

Below, a more prosaic but equally splendid view showing a typical Stockport tram in its home surroundings, this time at the foot of Lancashire Hill in Tiviot Dale. The wonderful pattern of the setts, the geometry of the tramlines and the careful positioning of the tram itself all make this arguably one of the most attractive scenes in the book. *(Neville Knight - MMC)*

Mersey Square continued to be busy with buses and trams jockeying for position whilst the imposing tower of the fire station continued to dominate the scene. The tempo would reduce now as one by one the tram routes were converted to bus operation – first the Hazel Grove to Crossley Road service in January 1950; next the cross town service from Edgeley to Vernon Park in March 1951, then Cheadle Heath to Mersey Square section of the Reddish route in April 1951.

There was still plenty of variety in the trams with three and four-window cars in service – note the multi-window platform vestibule on the car with its surfing conductor. Car 80, top, was working the service to Hazel Grove while the cross town service cars still loaded in the Square.

The end of the Cheadle service also meant an end to the wonderful view from Wellington Road bridge, opposite, where a selection of North Western's buses were lined up for inspection. *(NDC all)*

Reddish Bull's Head terminus, looking towards Gorton in August 1950. *(RWA Jones)*

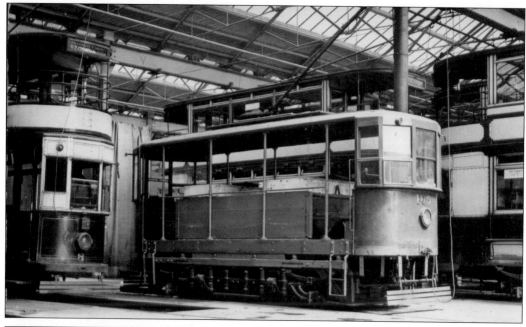

Stockport retained its veteran works cars to the end – unlike Bolton for instance where the snow plough was scrapped to make room in the depot, only for the worst blizzards in memory to close some lines for days on end soon afterwards!

The water car, above, had gained some protection for its crew, with windscreens, but the sides remained open to the elements. The late Gwynne Thomas recounted driving this car – in his school days and on a day out from Bolton – and overshooting the straight section of the loop by a foot or so, thereby blocking the line for any approaching car. He quietly set back, but gave a robust clout to a contractor's lorry standing close behind.

The lorry driver dashed round and apologised profusely – he thought his foot had slipped off the clutch and that he had gone forward. No damage was done and both vehicles went about their business.

Later that morning an Inspector enquired of the water car's crew if they knew anything about a large quantity of sand in the road at said loop. It transpired that the impact had dislodged a small mountain of sand from the underside of the lorry, completely blocking the tram line. Not that anyone was admitting anything of course . . .

Car 101, brought out for an enthusiast's visit, was formerly number 26. This view clearly shows the offset trolleypole mentioned in the early text as being necessary to allow cars to pass beneath the low railway bridges. *(MMC all)*

The decision to seek to abandon the trams meant, of course, that additional buses would be required over-and-above those included on the received tender. In the light of this the following decisions were made :-

1. To accept the Leyland tender for 24 buses complete at a cost of £3,585 each, this being the lowest price received.
2. To increase the order to 50 vehicles .
3. To request the Borough Council to approve the borrowing powers required.

At the March meeting of the Borough Council no decision was reached on the abandonment of the tramway, but, in connection with the proposal to increase the order for new buses from 24 to 50, a letter had been received from Crossley Motors objecting to this without the invitation of further tenders. Similar letters were received from the Amalgamated Engineering Union and from the National Union of Sheet Metal Workers and Brazers on behalf of their members at the Crossley Works. This resulted in the Council reversing the previous decision and instructing the Transport Committee, at its meeting on 14th March, to order only 24 Leyland buses. Since there had been no final decision regarding tramway abandonment no decision was reached regarding borrowing.

In June the Transport Committee took some comfort during the delay on the tramways' future by agreeing to a price increase of £13 per bus for the provision of Dunlopillo seating.

At the March meeting, as instructed, the Transport Committee agreed to the issue of tenders for a further 24 double-deck vehicles which would need financing. This was agreed by the Council at its June meeting when the decision was also made to abandon the tramway system.

Application for the loan was made to the Ministry of Transport, but the Ministry's reply asked why the application was for £280,000 for 48 buses? Who was it that couldn't count?

When tenders were received, the lowest was from Crossley Motors in the sum of £3,540 per vehicle which must have brought some relief to the Council as it avoided the political embarrassment of not placing the order with Crossley.

Manchester Piccadilly in 1948, with one of the Corporation's new Leylands setting the scene. Manchester numbered its buses in blocks by type at this time; Leyland double-deckers were all in the 3000 series, with Crossleys in 2000 and Daimlers in 4000 sequences. Two Stockport trams hide a very dismal-looking Manchester streamline-liveried bus in the background. *(NDC)*

Leyland's bus design was undoubtedly still in the top league and Stockport's fleet of these fine vehicles became well-known and admired in their smart red and white livery. Number 271 was from the first batch of PD2s, delivered in 1949 *(STA)*

It was rare indeed that a double-decker bus overturned and when it did happen it was, naturally, the source of interest for the local populace. Here 1946 Crossley number 240 has come to grief at Brinksway. Recovery will be a tricky operation for the breakdown crew. *(STA)*

(Courtesy A McK)

From the November meeting of the Transport Committee an estimate was sent to the Finance Committee which was to form the basis of the loan application. The figures were :-

24 Leyland double-deckers on order at £3,585 each	£86,040
Additional cost for Dunlopillo seating	£312
Cost of 24 Crossley double deckers at £3,540 each	£84,960
Total	£171,312

The Ministry gave approval to the loan application by January 1950, and the order was placed. The vehicles subsequently materialised as fleet numbers 285-308 – Leylands and numbers 309-32 – Crossleys.

Paul Abell, one of our contributors, travelled daily from Reddish to school at Cheadle Hulme in the 1960s and recalls that a Leyland on the number 17 service always seemed noticeably quicker than a Crossley – and left him more time to cross Mersey Square to catch the North Western bus to Cheadle Hulme.

In the meantime the tramway between Hazel Grove and Crossley Road had ceased on 14th January 1950, the cross town route between Edgeley and Vernon Park had ceased on 3rd March 1951 and the Stockport to Cheadle Heath section of the Reddish to Cheadle Heath service had ceased on 10th April 1951.

Also in April 1950, an offer was received from Laycock Engineering Ltd to fit a Laycock-Neale air power braking system, free of charge, to one of the Crossleys, and as Crossley Motors and the Stockport GM had no objection, the offer was accepted. The vehicle concerned was No. 332 and the system was retained until the winter of 1961-2 when it was replaced by vacuum braking.

In view of the tram service withdrawals mentioned above, work was put in hand to convert the tram portion of Heaton Lane depot for bus usage, but the work had not been completed when the new buses were ready for delivery. In December 1950 Crossley was storing its vehicles and in February 1951 terms were agreed with Leyland for the storage of vehicles manufactured by them.

A letter from Crossley was read at the Transport Committee meeting held on 18th June 1951 stating that they wanted to impose an additional charge of £46 13s 1d per chassis and £62 11s 5d per body, which would of course have raised the price above the Leylands. The matter was resolved by reference to the Borough Treasurer but the actual outcome is not clear.

Deliveries eventually began in 1951 and were complete in time for the final abandonment of the tramway with the withdrawal of the Reddish service on 12th August 1951.

The final closure came when car number 82 performed the last duty, followed by ceremonial cars 57 and 53, thus bringing to an end 50 years to the day of tramcar operation in Stockport. Number 53 was decorated for the occasion and carried the Mayor, members of the Town Council and others from Mersey Square to Reddish and back. Driver Jim Ball was the official 'last tram driver'. Mr William Henry Bowers of Stockport was one of the passengers on the town's first tramcar. Now, 50 years later, Mr Bowers made the journey from Mersey Square to Reddish and back on the tramcar thus giving him a unique achievement as a passenger.

Local tramway historian and author Ian Yearsley was also a passenger on the last tramcar, and wrote in his book *The Manchester Tram*:- 'And now it was Stockport's turn. Stockport, whose trams had outlasted everyone else's in this part of the country. It seemed hard to imagine a tramless Stockport, yet it was only a few hours away'.

On the following morning the replacement number 17 bus made its way to Reddish from Mersey Square whilst dismantling of the overhead commenced in the Square itself. As mentioned much earlier, a moment of drama had occurred when the 'new' Dennis tower wagon purchased in 1938 had overturned just a little earlier, and the veteran Dennis from 1915 was left to get on with the work.

Stockport was fond of its veterans; tucked away in the garage was another strange beast, a Karrier used as a tow wagon but which had in its first life been a Shell petrol tanker way back in 1926. With no front wheel brakes, and

somewhat ineffective ones on the rear, it must have been a mobile nightmare when loaded with petrol and in daily use. It wasn't withdrawn until 1970 and must surely rank as the strangest vehicle the PTE had inherited. It survives as a museum piece in the Boyle Street collection, having been restored by courtesy of Nuclear Fuels Ltd.

With the withdrawal of the trams and other associated paraphernalia from a (very) distant age, the Stockport fleet now numbered 164 buses, and included 34 prewar vehicles, 21 wartime vehicles and 109 postwar vehicles. Apart from the withdrawal of one single-decker in 1952, the fleet would then remain unchanged until 1958.

Facing page: The end of the tramway was marked in traditional fashion with an illuminated car – number 53. Whilst time-consuming in fixing the strings of light bulb holders, the provision of power to light them was, of course, an easy matter with over 500 volts available from the overhead supply. Dignitaries, staff and enthusiasts mix in these two views which really did mark the end of an era.

The nearest trams would now be found in Liverpool or Blackpool, or, over the hills in Leeds. The heady days of travelling to local or more distant towns from Stockport by trams from different undertakings had finally come to an end. *(MMC both)*

When the vehicle audit was carried out by the PTE there may well have been some raised eyebrows – a Karrier, well yes, but built in 1926 – surely not? But there was no mistake, and here it is. Purchased by Stockport by 1935 it became No. 106 in the service fleet.

Fitted with a 5-litre petrol engine and registered in London as YM 9410, the mark it still carries, it operated for Shell. A contemporary trade advert for a similar tanker-bodied Karrier, but operating for Texaco, gives some idea how it would have looked. Still on original solid tyres, with a clutch which is either **in** or **out** and brakes which are not of any great value, it finds little to endear it to the Museum staff who are happy to let sleeping dogs lie – especially this one. *(STA)*

The first batch of post-war buses arrived in 1946 and was similar to the final undelivered pre-war Crossley No. 207 (see page 89) which had arrived earlier that year. They comprised 20 more all-Crossley vehicles and the first, No. 225 (JA 7625) is pictured here on Woodbank Estate, a mere 12 minutes run from Mersey Square and the terminus of service 38 which had commenced in 1957. This was one of a number of local town routes where the journey time from the town centre was less than 15 minutes. *(STA)*

In 1949 Stockport once more purchased double-deckers from Leyland, a batch of 20 PD2/1s arriving that year. Stockport's application of their livery, complete with lining out, suited these Leyland bodies very well. Number 277 (DJA 185) is about to leave Mersey Square for Adswood, another of the short routes which would see this bus back in the town centre within 30 minutes. *(STA)*

In order to replace the final trams, Stockport placed its biggest single order for motorbuses ever, for no less than 48 buses. These arrived in 1951 and were split equally between two manufacturers and included the final bodies from Leyland, fitted to 24 more Leyland PD2s which were numbered 285 to 308. Such was the reliability of the Leylands that a majority of them passed to SELNEC PTE in 1969, including No. 293 (EDB 547), seen above. *(STA)*

The balance of the order went to the local firm of Crossley and was fitted with their own bodywork on their DD42/7 chassis, as exemplified by No 324 (EDB 578). Immediately after leaving this stop the vehicle will start the steep climb to St Peter's Square, and if the driver is not able to get into second gear before starting the climb it will be a long slow crawl to the top. No Crossley buses were passed by Stockport to the PTE. *(RM)*

Buses reign supreme now. North Western's rebodying programme is under way, with two Willowbrook double-deckers in the foreground; one of its Leyland-bodied Titans stands outside the Transport Offices. The inevitable English Electric-bodied single-decker is almost hidden in front of the crowd boarding number 207 in the centre of this view, (identifiable since it was the only post-war double-decker bus with a nearside destination display) whilst another makes its way up Wellington Road in the distance. At least five of the other buses are Stockport Crossley double-deckers. (STA)

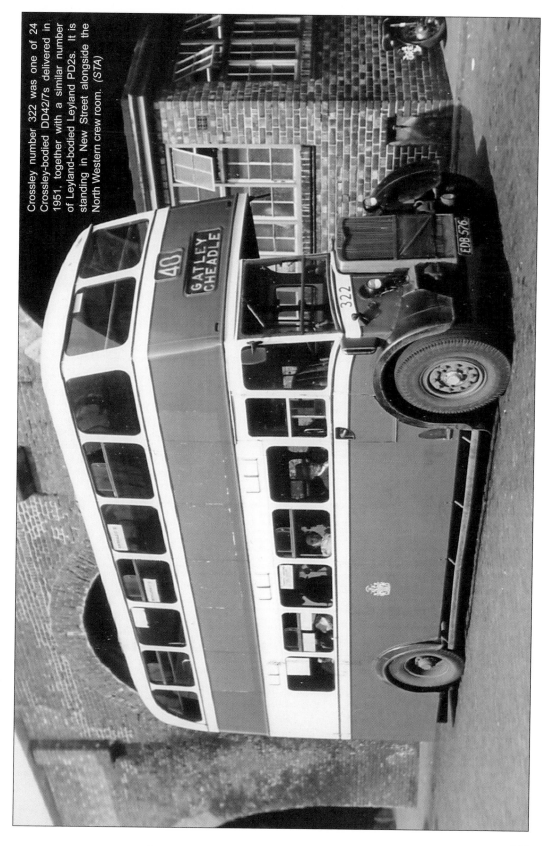

Crossley number 322 was one of 24 Crossley-bodied DD42/7s delivered in 1951, together with a similar number of Leyland-bodied Leyland PD2s. It is standing in New Street alongside the North Western crew room. (STA)

16 – Events in the 1950s

The provision of new buses did not appear again on the agenda of the Transport Committee until June 1955 when the Chairman made reference to the need to replace a number of time expired vehicles and proposed that twelve new double-deckers and four new single-deckers be purchased. The matter was deferred until September 1955 when the Chairman reported the need to replace the 20 centre-entrance single-deckers which had been used for works services to Bird Hall Lane where a low bridge had prohibited the use of double-deckers. There was, however, a proposal from Cheadle and Gatley Urban District Council to lower the road under the bridge thus removing the restriction. In the light of this it was agreed that tenders be invited for ten double-deckers and four saloons.

The Transport Committee agreed the specification for these vehicles but when the undertaking's Joint Works Committee was consulted they suggested that the width for these next deliveries should be 8ft, not 7ft 6ins. In mid-November the Transport Committee agreed the alterations suggested by the Works Committee with the exception of the change in width. An opposition party proposal to accept the 8ft width was defeated but later the full Council refused to agree the 7ft 6ins width and the Transport Committee had to specify the width of 8ft 0ins.

Having finally agreed matters, in a situation worthy of the best Vaudeville pantomime came a communication from the Ministry. Never mind the width, what about the length?

This letter from the Ministry of Transport was considered on 2nd February 1956, advising that from 1st June 1956, double-deck buses on 2 axles and 30ft long would be legal.

This apparently appealed to some members of the Committee, and considerable discussion followed but as was so often the case no decision was reached. One can see how Mr Wroth might well have despaired at such tactics in his days in charge, contrasting it with North Western where there were no committees and Councillors to circumnavigate. However, at the next meeting, the Town Clerk advised that the money available had been reduced to £70,000 and the Committee agreed to invite tenders for ten double-deckers 27ft 6ins x 8ft and four single-deckers 30ft x 8ft.

Almost all of the 1936/7 Leyland TS7/8s lasted into the 1960s, the last (No. 200) not being withdrawn until 1963. Below No. 189 (JA 7599) is in use on driver training duties. Opposite, No. 196 (JA 7596) is seen on cross-town service 75, a regular haunt of these single-deckers until it became double-deck operated, as a result of which they were finally withdrawn, having well and truly earned their keep. *(STA; KWS)*

One of the distinctively shaped TD3s of which number 166 was the second, being delivered in 1934, is shown here at Kingsway, awaiting its return journey to Reddish. These two V-fronted models were both withdrawn in 1958. In the background can be seen the clock tower, all that now remains of the former Manchester Corporation Transport Parrs Wood Garage which later became the Selnec Parcels depot. After another reincarnation the site was developed by Tesco. *(AEJ)*

Number 170 and its fellows from the next batch of Leylands (171-8) was a TD4c and was still in service but approaching the end of its life when this photograph was taken on the A6 road alongside Mersey Square at the 92 Manchester to Hazel Grove bus stop. It has lost the *Gearless Bus* lettering, and its torque convertor equipment. It was withdrawn in 1959 but even then passed into C Holt of Rusholme contractor's fleet for more work. *(STA)*

Crossley number 203 being overtaken by a rather nippy North Western Road Car Co Ltd Weymann-bodied Leyland PD2 leaving Stockport for Altrincham on the 80 service, one of two services operating between the two towns at that time. *(AEJ)*

The other Mancunian, 205 also dating from 1941, was photographed in April 1953, and as mentioned in the text, was one of three Crossley double-deckers ordered to be allocated numbers 203, 205 and 207. The two wartime examples were withdrawn in 1958. Immediately behind No. 205 in Mersey Square is an area known as 'The Bear Pit'. In its heyday it was used for political and other meetings, where one George Brown MP famously encountered some flying eggs. The indicator settings are designed to confuse the uninitiated, for the 39 departed from the side of the New Street arches by the flight of steps down from Wellington Road. *(RM)*

Tenders were received in June 1956 but this time no decision was reached pending a review of the method of financing. In October the Finance and Rating Committee finally approved the purchase of 14 vehicles at a cost of £29,355 9s. 11d for the Leyland chassis and £36,190 for bodies by Crossley, both of these tenders being the lowest received.

The single-deckers arrived in June 1958 and the double-deckers in July 1958 numbered 333-42. It had originally been intended to number the vehicles 333-46 but it was then decided to number single-deckers in a separate series commencing at 400, but not before the first of the single-deckers had arrived with its original number; only the last, number 403, did not have to be renumbered. Thus Leyland PD2s numbered 343-6 became 333-6 shortly after entering service. Double-decker 335 (originally 345) carried the last Crossley bus body to be built. The last passenger bodies were on the Glasgow trolleybuses, though some were completed at Park Royal after Errwood Park was closed.

Bus services were developed to serve new housing estates – a local service to Bridge Hall Estate in May 1952 and another to Woodbank Estate in November 1957. There was a long running feud with North Western Road Car

Bodywork on some of the ten 1958 Crossley-bodied Leyland PD2s is believed to have been completed by SCTD staff after the closure of the Crossley works was announced, causing delivery delays. Number 334, (delivered as 344,) was photographed in October 1961, by which time the terminus for the number 18 service had moved to Chorlton Street, Manchester as seen above.

Within a few years a multi-storey car park was built over the bus bays, thereby at a stroke replicating the gloomy ambience of the infamous Greengate Arches in Salford. Part of the site is still in use today for National Express services – though thankfully considerably upgraded! *(RM)*

Facing page: With the completion of the 1951 deliveries, Stockport was well equipped with modern vehicles and no further purchases were made until 1958. By that time Crossley had ceased manufacture of chassis and Leyland had ceased manufacture of bus bodies. An order was placed for ten Leyland PD2/30 chassis and with Crossley Motors for bodywork. At this time Crossley was part of the ACV Group and produced bodies to a Park Royal design. An attractive well finished body was produced but they were the last bus bodies to be built at the Crossley works in Stockport prior to closure. The attractive well proportioned lines of the body are illustrated in this view of No. 337 at West Didsbury on service 9. They were fitted with the current Leyland design of full width bonnet often referred to as the 'tin front' and designed originally to meet the requirements of Midland Red. *(NDC)*

123

Most of the routes terminating in Stockport did so in Mersey Square. Among the exceptions were routes to Cheadle, Gatley and Councillor Lane which terminated here in New Street, by the arches carrying the elevated section of the A6. (KWS)

Facing page and above: The Titan TD4c vehicles, numbers 171-8, gave very good service and the final five, 174-8, were not withdrawn until 1960. The last of the batch is shown opposite in New Street on 16th March 1957, the valuable space under the arches being put to good use by the Corporation Cleansing Department. The arch behind the bus is the one under which the trams ran to Cheadle, using the interlaced track. In the view above, number 176 is seen making a smoky start from Heaton Lane depot on learner duties. *(KWS; STA)*

Company Limited regarding a service to a new estate at Brinnington between Stockport and Denton and also regarding express services from Cheadle Hulme to Manchester but these were eventually settled.

The battle over the Brinnington service had arisen because Stockport Council had, in its infinite wisdom, chosen to build extensive new council housing alongside the Denton Road, which had been served by North Western's exclusive service 81 to Denton. Initially, a joint service numbered 81a to the Farmers Arms had commenced by 1959, but these were augmented by new joint services 54 and 55 to Brinnington, although not before another last-minute hiccup had delayed their eventual introduction in 1963. Despite the battle fought by the company to secure its share of this development, this did not prevent North Western from abandoning the operation to the

Corporation on busy summer Saturdays in the late 1960s, when both buses and crews were diverted to cover the company's extensive longer-distance service requirements.

The long-deferred matter of worn-out vehicles, first raised way back in 1955, now arose again when the General Manager had reported to the June 1957 Transport Committee meeting on the condition of time expired buses, some of which were 20 years old, and recommended the purchase of ten new double-deckers.

By September, eleven tenders had been received. The lowest tenders were from Leyland Motors for the chassis at £22,648 4s 2d and from Longwell Green Coachworks, Bristol for the bodies in the sum of £25,850. This would be the first time that Longwell Green had supplied bodies to the North West of England.

The Longwell Green Leylands lasted in PTE days, outliving the Department, and could be seen in Glossop passing the Publisher's then-offices working the jointly-operated long number 6 route to Manchester after transfer to Manchester's Hyde Road depot. Back in 1958, however, the question of financing of these vehicles was discussed and the Transport Committee suggested to the Finance and Rating Committee that the Transport Reserve Fund be used. This was left over from tramway days and as it had no further use the suggestion was agreed.

Delivery began in February 1960 and the rather distinctive buses were numbered 343-52.

Also delivered in 1958 were four Leyland Tiger Cub model PSUC1/1 underfloor engined single-deckers – Stockport's first example of this type of vehicle. The bodies were by Crossley and as explained in the text they were renumbered 400 to 403 to segregate single and double-deckers. The first three were altered within a few days of entering service but the last, 403 never operated as 336. The moulding around the Tiger Cub badge bears a striking resemblance to that fitted to the contemporary AEC/Park Royal Monocoach from ACV.

Number 400 is shown above, about to leave the former tram section of Heaton Lane depot whilst below No. 403 is shown loading in Mersey Square. Although showing Offerton on the indicator, it was actually heading in the opposite direction towards Green Lane's terminus of service 75. *(STA both)*

Facing page: This time actually loading for Offerton on service 75 in April 1960 is Crossley-bodied Leyland PSUC1/1 number 402, originally delivered as No. 335. When new these vehicles had totally enclosed cabs but they were soon modified to just floor-to-waist level with an access door into the driver's area. *(RM)*

By 1960 neither Leyland nor Crossley were building bus bodies, so it was evident that Stockport's 10 double-deck deliveries that year, still on Leyland PD2 chassis, were to see a new manufacturer's products enter the fleet. It turned out to be Longwell Green Coachworks, a builder named after the suburb of Bristol in which it was based. The company had been associated with South Wales municipal operators, but no orders had previously been received from the North West. It has been suggested that the bodies were based on frames manufactured and supplied by HV Burlingham of Blackpool, and certainly the bodies had more than a passing resemblance to their products. The views on this page and the next show three examples of the batch; No. 343 (above) on service 20 at Heaton Lane *en route* from Woodford to Manchester; No. 347 (below) on service 31 at Ashton bus station and No. 344 (opposite) entering Albert Square, Manchester on service 89 and about to pass Manchester's impressive Town Hall. Stockport's routes were nothing if not ubiquitous. *(STA; RM; STA)*

Early 1962 was a noteworthy time for the undertaking, when a further 10 Leyland PD2s entered service, with bodywork by a supplier who was to remain the Council's choice for the remainder of its existence, namely East Lancashire Coachbuilders. The batch also saw the replacement of the 'Midland Red' style full-width bonnet by the fibreglass 'St Helens' style, making them PD2A/30 models. Number 356 (VDB 586) is seen here outside Mersey Square depot. The lower view, at the same spot, shows Longwell Green-bodied Leyland, No. 347 (PJA 917), photographed during the late 1960s, passing the former site of the Transport depot in Mersey Square, now demolished with the early stages of the building of the Merseyway Shopping Precinct in progress. *(RM; RGR)*

(Courtesy A McK)

Shipshape and Bristol fashion – surely a suitable epithet for a new Longwell Green vehicle, gleaming as this one certainly did? It was standing on the A6 adjacent to Heaton Lane garage having completed a short working of the 20 service and terminating in Stockport. *(RM)*

The war-time Guy Arabs were to serve their owners well; it was not until 1963 that the first were withdrawn. Above, No. 221 (JA 7621), was photographed much earlier than this in 1954 when it was still almost a 'front-line' vehicle. Number 213 (JA 7613), on the other hand, was approaching its last days in service and was setting off for Parrs Wood on the 26, a short-working of the joint 16 service. Despite its age, the body shows no signs of the need for rebuilding, which was often the case with utility bodies. *(RM; HP)*

16 – 1960s: The Final Years

By the early 1960s Leyland's rear-engined Atlantean chassis was becoming a fairly common sight amongst many big fleet operators, and the Daimler Fleetline and Guy Wulfrunian models were also offering engineers various challenges. Traffic Managers were quick to see the advantages of more seats and better passenger control and safety with an enclosed front door.

The Unions took a different view, with capacity approaching 90 passengers when some operators were still using 56-seat vehicles with five standing. The fact that some large bogie trams had carried numbers approaching 100 was quietly ignored. It should also be pointed out that this was a time when the major transport unions were jockeying for position, trying to increase their membership numbers and, therefore, influence. Collateral damage to small matters such as the introduction of rear-engined buses was, perforce, of secondary importance.

Stockport's conservative attitude to new bus design was, however, to be applauded, for the Atlantean in its early form was far from trouble-free. Strong union resistance in Manchester meant that the fleet of new buses – dubbed 'Red Dragons' – stood rejected and idle in the Hyde Road garage for many months before terms for their use were eventually hammered out.

In the light of this and other developments, when it was decided in April 1960 to invite tenders for the next ten double-deckers it was also confirmed that they would be to similar specification to those recently delivered, in other words with the engine at the front.

Thus although the Leyland Atlantean rear engined double-decker was available, it was the majority decision to continue with traditional vehicles.

When it came to decision time the choice of Leyland chassis came as no surprise, but what was surprising was the acceptance of the tender from East Lancashire Coachbuilders Ltd at £2,289 each as the lowest 'according to the Department's specification'. East Lancashire had a good reputation as a supplier to municipal fleets and the department would have no cause to regret the choice. Delivery of these vehicles was complete

Manchester bought some of the early Atlanteans, bodied by Metro-Cammell in Birmingham, as seen here. It was felt by many that their design was uninspiring, though there had been many far worse examples on front-engined chassis – East Lancashire gaining business in Southampton after perhaps the worst-ever designed AECs entered service there. Manchester then moved the goal posts and the *avant-garde* second generation Mancunians later took to the road. *(JAS)*

133

One of the 1962 Leylands, No. 354 (VDB 585), is about to leave the sombre surroundings of Heaton Lane depot. The East Lancs bodies must have been satisfactory; the following year another 10 buses with the same combination were obtained. After 262 consecutively numbered buses, however, Mr Brimelow, the new General Manager, determined that the fleet numbering would re-commence at 1, an exercise he had carried out at SHMD, and in Stockport was fortunate enough to obtain matching registration marks. By the time this photograph of number 2 (YDB 2), was taken, the Merseyway Shopping Precinct was open for business and the days of the Corporation buses were almost at an end. *(STA both)*

COUNTY BOROUGH OF
STOCKPORT
PASSENGER TRANSPORT DEPT.
1886

JANUARY, 1960

OFFICIAL

TIME TABLES
AND FARES TABLES

TRANSPORT OFFICES
MERSEY SQUARE
STOCKPORT

PRICE
6d.

SERVICE No. 92 — HAZEL GROVE, STOCKPORT and MANCHESTER

(Operated jointly by Manchester and Stockport Corporations).

MONDAY TO SATURDAY

	am	am	am	am	am	am	am	am	am	am		pm	pm	pm
Hazel Grove	—	5 15	5 31	5 43	5 55	6 7	—	6 19	—	6 31	and	7 1	7 8	7 15
Stockport (Mersey Square)	4 59	5 30	5 46	5 58	6 10	6 22	6 28	6 34	6 40	6 46	every	7 16	7 23	7 30
Levenshulme (Lloyd Road)	5 7	5 36	5 54	6 6	6 18	6 30	6 36	6 42	6 48	6 54	6	7 24	7 31	7 38
Ardwick Green	—	5 49	6 10	6 22	6 34	6 46	6 52	6 58	7 4	7 10	mins.	7 40	7 47	7 54
Manchester (Piccadilly)	—	5 57	6 17	6 29	6 41	6 53	6 59	7 5	7 11	7 17	until	7 47	7 54	8 1

	pm	pm		pm	pm	pm	pm	pm	pm	pm	pm	pm	pm	pm
Hazel Grove	7 23	7 30	and at	10 8	1015	1023	1030	1038	1045	1053	110	11 8	1115	1120
Stockport (Mersey Square)	7 38	7 45	similar	1023	1030	1038	1045	1053	110	11 8	1115	1123	1130	1135
Levenshulme (Lloyd Road)	7 46	7 53	inter-	1031	1038	1046	1053	111	11 8	—	—	—	—	—
Ardwick Green	8 2	8 9	vals	1047	1053	11 2	—	—	—	—	—	—	—	—
Manchester (Piccadilly)	8 9	8 16	until	1054	—	—	—	—	—	—	—	—	—	—

53

	am	am	am	am	am	am	am	am	am	am	am	pm	pm	pm
Manchester (Piccadilly)	...	—	—	—	—	5 28	5 40	—	5 52	—	6 4	—	6 16	
Ardwick Green	...	—	—	—	—	5 35	5 47	—	5 59	—	6 11	—	6 23	
Levenshulme (Lloyd Road)	...	—	5 7	—	—	5 51	6 3	—	6 15	—	6 27	—	6 39	
Stockport (Mersey Square)	...	4 59	5 15	5 23	5 35	5 47	5 59	6 11	6 17	6 23	6 29	6 35	6 41	6 47
Hazel Grove	...	5 15	5 31	5 39	5 51	6 3	6 15	6 27	6 39	6 45	6 51	6 57	7 3	

	am	am	am	am	am		pm	pm	pm	pm	pm		pm
Manchester (Piccadilly)	...	—	6 28	—	6 40	6 46	and	6 53	6 56	7 0	7 8	715 and at	1023
Ardwick Green	...	—	6 35	—	6 47	6 53	every	7 0	7 3	7 7	7 15	722 similar	1030
Levenshulme (Lloyd Road)	...	—	6 51	—	7 3	7 9	6	7 16	7 19	7 21	7 29	736 inter-	1044
Stockport (Mersey Square)	...	6 53	6 59	7 5	7 11	7 17	mins.	7 23	7 26	7 30	7 38	745 vals	1053
Hazel Grove	...	7 9	7 15	7 21	7 27	7 33	until	7 39	—	7 46	7 54	8 1 until	11 9

	pm	pm	pm	pm	pm	pm	pm	pm	pm
Manchester (Piccadilly)	1030	—	1038	—	1045	—	1053	110	—
Ardwick Green	1037	—	1045	—	1052	—	110	117	—
Levenshulme (Lloyd Road)	1051	1052	1059	115	116	1112	1114	1121	—
Stockport (Mersey Square)	—	110	—	1113	—	1120	—	—	—
Hazel Grove	—	1116	—	—	—	—	—	—	—

(NDC two;
AMK below)

Manchester & Stockport Corporation Transport Departments.

STOCKPORT (Bramhall Moor Lane) & MANCHESTER (Chorlton St.)

Service No. 18.

Commencing on Monday, 27th. July 1959, the journey from Stockport (Bramhall Moor Lane) at 6-5p.m. will terminate at Albert Road, Levenshulme, instead of Chorlton Street Bus Station.

Above, in an interesting comparison with the view on page 3, No. 10 (YDB 10), of the 1963 deliveries is seen climbing out of Mersey Square to St Peter's Square. Below, number 21, (BJA 921B) shows the improvement by reverting to exposed radiators on the department's Leyland Titans. *(STA: AEJ)*

by April 1962 and they received fleet Nos. 353-62. They were well-proportioned, and well finished, and most importantly they were built to meet what Stockport wanted. As a result this firm was to become the sole supplier of bodies to the Department for the remainder of its existence.

In 1962, Mr Eric Booth Baxter, the General Manager, retired after serving in this capacity for 24 years. He was succeeded by Mr Frank S Brimelow, who had entered the industry as a junior clerk with Warrington Corporation Transport Department in 1931, quickly becoming Chief Clerk in 1933. Following war service, he returned to Warrington as Chief Assistant to the General Manager and then in 1950 he moved to become Deputy General Manager at Middlesbrough Corporation Transport Department. From 1957 to 1962 he was General Manager at the Stalybridge, Hyde, Mossley and Dukinfield Joint Transport Board.

Joint operation with other operators had been a feature for many years, some of these joint services involving North Western, Ashton Corporation, SHMD and Manchester Corporation. The variety of operators meant an interesting selection of makes and liveries could be seen in Mersey Square and the surrounding area.

When Mr Brimelow arrived in 1963 he found that even with the steady renewal policy

The next delivery of Leylands arriving in 1964 reverted to exposed radiators (as would all subsequent double-deckers), and were PD2/40 models, totalling 15 in number. They were the first buses in the fleet to carry registration marks with a suffix letter, Stockport Council having reverted to registration marks commencing with 'A' for this purpose. Number. 17 (BJA 917B) is seen above crossing Mersey Square with Merseyway closed off at the extreme left. *(RM)*

implemented the fleet still contained 22 prewar and wartime vehicles, together with 65 Crossley DD42 models, dating from 1946 to 1951, which were showing their age and for which spares were becoming increasingly difficult to obtain. Having been in charge at the neighbouring SHMD undertaking this could hardly have come as a surprise but the responsibility to rectify matters was now his.

It was therefore at the April 1963 Transport Committee Meeting, the first Mr Brimelow attended, that he reported on the fleet condition with the recommendation that four single-deckers and 73 double-deckers be replaced over the next five years by purchasing 15 double-deckers per year and the new single-deckers at the earliest opportunity.

This proposal was approved and tenders were invited for 15 double-deckers and four single-

Towards the end of their lives, it was not unusual for certain buses to be relegated to training duties. Numerically the last Leyland-bodied PD2 to be delivered, No. 308 (EDB 562) has here been awarded this honour. Seen passing the almost now complete Merseyway Shopping Precinct, it duly found its way into the ranks of preserved vehicles. *(RM)*

deckers. Matters moved quickly; the tenders were returned by 22nd June 1963 and orders were placed with Leyland for chassis and East Lancashire Coachbuilders for bodies. These were the lowest tenders received, and the chassis would revert to the exposed radiator type. The question of the single-deckers was deferred until October when Mr Brimelow reported that double-deckers had been substituted for single-deckers on the 75 route between Green End and Offerton and this had resulted in the disposal of the remaining prewar single-deckers without their needing to be replaced at that time. There had always been unease about putting double-deckers on this route because of the tilt on the very sharp right uphill turn from Wellington Road into Middle Hillgate.

The new double-deckers, numbered 11 to 25, arrived in 1964 and their arrival led to the withdrawal of the last eight wartime Guy Arabs which had given almost 20 years of service, quite an achievement for wartime vehicles without rebodying or any signs of major rebuilding.

Mr Brimelow's stay as General Manager was short before he moved to the other side of the County of Cheshire to become General Manager of the larger Birkenhead Corporation Transport but he had ensured the continuation of the Department's high standard in vehicle selection.

He was succeeded by a former employee of the Department, Mr Harold Eaton, who had been Traffic Superintendent from 1945 to 1951 before moving to Accrington Corporation Transport Department as General Manager, a position which he held until returning to Stockport in 1964.

Mr Eaton was to be the last General Manager of the Department and with the formation of SELNEC, became Traffic Manager, Southern Division.

In April 1964, in furtherance of the agreed policy, Mr Eaton was authorised to invite tenders for a further 15 double-deckers and in October approval was once again given for orders to be placed with Leyland for chassis and with East Lancashire Coachbuilders for bodies, and these arrived in 1965 becoming numbers 26-40.

Twelve months later, in April 1965, the Transport Committee authorised the invitation of tenders for a further 15 double-deckers but in July of the same year, the General Manager reported on the current poor delivery situation and recommended that the tenders be revised to cover 30 vehicles.

Cause and effect . . . . *(AMcK)*

Number 226 (JA 7626) was the first of its batch to be withdrawn apparently following an abortive trip through the arch below Wellington Road. Although the trams had been withdrawn, the ears to which the overhead wires had been attached were still in place and the bus roof was very neatly sliced open, fortunately with no passengers aboard at the time. Minus roof, it was subsequently retained for a variety of duties, including tree-lopping, driver training and route equipment duties. It was sold as a potential preservation project, but finally dismantled for spares, the engine being installed in a restored Sunderland Crossley double-decker. The lower picture was taken in March 1968 in connection with the diversion of certain services via Exchange Street and a window-bill announcing this change is shown above. *(STA: RGR)*

This was agreed, and at the October Transport Committee Meeting it was resolved that yet again orders be placed with Leyland for chassis and with East Lancashire Coachbuilders for bodies, these again being the lowest quotes received.

Fifteen of the bodies were actually built to East Lancashire design at Neepsend Coachworks in Sheffield, an associate company of East Lancashire Coachbuilders, both being, at that time, part of the Cravens Group. The vehicles arrived in 1967 and were numbered 41-55 with East Lancashire bodies, and 56-70 with Neepsend bodies.

The regular pattern was broken the following year, for at the April 1966 Transport Committee Meeting authorisation was given to invite tenders for 15 double-deckers, and five single-deckers equipped for one-person-operation. The major specification change was that the double-deckers were to be 30ft long.

Tenders were accepted in July 1966 and again the double-deck chassis were to be supplied by Leyland at a cost of £2,800 16s 8d and the bodies by East Lancashire Coachbuilders at a cost of £3,745 each – prices were creeping up steadily. Orders for the single-deckers were placed with the same manufacturers at a cost of £2,573 13s 6d for the chassis and £3,380 for the bodies.

These were not the lowest tenders but were described as being 'the most suitable' and few who knew the fleet would argue with that assessment. The vehicles arrived in 1968, the double-decker PD3s being numbered 71-85 and the single-decker Leopards 404-8.

Their arrival brought to an end the five years substantial rolling stock replacement programme introduced by Mr Brimelow when he became General Manager in 1963, and also saw the departure of the last of the Crossleys – two significant milestones.

On the services side, a new joint service to Manchester commenced in 1967 via Green End and Kingsway.

Delivered in 1968 were five Leyland Leopards with East Lancs bodies designed for one-man-operation, Nos. 404-8 (KDB 404-8F); the winds of change were at last wafting through the undertaking. Number 408 negotiates Mersey Square with both doors open, an event that would cause palpitations in today's Health & Safety circles, but it has to be remembered that in 1968 doors were a distinctly rare feature on Stockport's buses. It will be observed that these buses brought centre-entrances back to service 75. The distinctive furniture storage building has now passed to Pickfords. *(STA)*

A further 15 Leylands arrived in 1965. A change in construction and use regulations has seen the trafficators moved closer to the front of the bus on these deliveries. When new on at least some of the batch, they were placed on the mudguards to ensure compliance; needless to say, they did not stay in this position too long as shown below. The first of the order, No. 26 (FDB 326C), demonstrates this feature, whilst, below, this time it is the turn of No.35 (FDB 335C), to be photographed 'underneath the arches' in New Street on the service 40 stand – see pages 117 and 124. *(STA; BD)*

No less than 30 of the by-now standard Leyland/East Lancs design were taken into stock in 1967. There were in fact two batches this year; Nos. 41-55 (HJA 941-55E) being standard products, but Nos. 56-70 (HJA 956-70E) actually had bodies built in Sheffield by Neepsend to East Lancs design, both companies at the time being part of the Craven group. Notice the indicators, now at the front above the cab, and the advert on No. 62; although still in Corporation livery the bus belongs to SELNEC PTE and staff recruitment is necessary. *(AEJ: BD)*

Although the wind of change was in the air, and the Transport Act's likely implications were becoming known, it was decided to maintain the rolling stock replacement programme and in April 1967 tenders were invited for another twelve double-deckers.

By this time the traditional rear-entrance front-engined double-decker was becoming rare, and alternative prices were requested for rear or forward-entrance bodywork. Once again Leyland submitted the lowest prices for chassis, these being £2,855 11s 2d for rear-entrance and £2,843 11s 2d for front-entrance, the lower price being accounted for by the fact that the forward-entrance vehicles did not require drop frames for the rear platform.

East Lancashire Coachbuilders quoted £3,765 for rear-entrance and £4,080 for front-entrance bodies. The not inconsiderable difference would be largely accounted for by the fitment of folding door equipment at the front. The rear-entrance price was not the lowest but was considered to be the most suitable, whilst the front-entrance price was the lowest.

In true bet-hedging manner, six rear-entrance and six forward-entrance vehicles were ordered from Leyland and East Lancashire Coachbuilders. The classic East Lancashire double-deck body for front engined chassis, which looked well in any livery, looked particularly good in Stockport's red

and off white attractive livery and gave its buses a quality look which was often lacking in other fleets at this time when a desire for economy sometimes led to the purchase of lightweight vehicles with spartan interior finish. One feature which Stockport retained to the end was the use of fluted leather covering to the seats at a time when some operators were using flat leather or some form of plastic covering.

During the 'fifties and the 'sixties, many operators introduced simpler liveries in an attempt to achieve economies, often resulting in a drab appearance. By contrast other operators introduced brighter liveries, particularly in the 'sixties in an attempt to improve the appearance of their vehicles. Stockport resisted the temptation to simplify their livery and as it was an attractive one there was no need to improve it. The Stockport double-deck paint scheme introduced

A further batch of 15 East Lancs-bodied Leylands entered service in 1968, but at last the department had embraced the by-now 12-year old regulations, and opted for the 30ft length of the PD3. Despite allegations on the destination blinds to the contrary, number 71 (KJA 871F), the first of the order, is heading back to Stockport and approaching 55, Piccadilly, Manchester's legendary head office. This vehicle is now one of the preserved Stockport buses, though in SELNEC colours. *(STA)*

with the first double-deckers in 1934 never dated and still looked attractive and up-to-date in 1969. The Leopard single-deckers of 1968 were an exception, of course, in their reversed livery as shown on page 140.

The next vehicles arrived in 1969, carrying numbers 86-97, and rear-entrance No. 91 became the last traditional rear entrance double-decker to enter service in the United Kingdom.

In June 1968 the Committee had been advised that gates could be provided for forward-entrance buses to close off the upper saloon and make them suitable for one-person-operation. Accordingly, the six forward-entrance buses were delivered with gates strapped beneath the stairs but these were never used and soon disappeared. One imagines they probably found a use as stair-gates of a different sort – in homes with young children!

In another wish-list item the nearside window of the driver's cab was angled to assist with one-person-operation but it is thought that because of union opposition they were not utilised this way.

The final deliveries came in 1969, when 12 more Leyland PD3s with East Lancs bodies arrived. Industry trends for some years had favoured the moving of the entrance position to the front of the bus to improve safety. At last Stockport recognised this, but in case the argument was not all that it seemed to be, split the order 50:50 between standard (rear) and novel (front) entrances just in case. On the facing page, number 86 (MJA 886) was representative of the former which were numbered 86-91 while, below, No. 97 (MJA 897G) was numerically the final bus delivered to Stockport. All of these passed to SELNEC PTE within a year. See also page 176 for another view of number 97 in its later life. *(RM; BD)*

17 – 1968/9 – Going down, but going down fighting

We have concentrated on matters in the Transport Department over the last decade or so, but Stockport was about to undergo a major change the likes of which could not have been dreamt of in earlier days. In a redevelopment of the town centre, Merseyway, the only section of dual-carriageway road in the borough, and opened in 1940, was to disappear under a vast new shopping precinct.

To allow this, the fire station was demolished and Mersey Square depot was replaced in early 1968 by a new maintenance depot and headquarters as part of the scheme. Heaton Lane garage was used to house a small collection of preserved vehicles for a while, and was also used by an independent contractor to fit radios to vehicles in the Selnec Southern fleet.

The 1968 Transport Act was not universally popular as all the transport assets (and liabilities) held by the constituent local authorities had to be handed over to the new Passenger Transport Executive with effect from 1st November 1969. Stockport was surrendering probably the most modern and up-to-date premises relinquished by any of the concerns involved.

The new engineering depot and office complex was based at Daw Bank immediately under the western side of the town centre railway viaduct and is still in use by Stagecoach today. Subsequently the Heaton Lane premises were also demolished. These actions apparently caused considerable friction with the finance division at the new PTE when it came into being.

The thinking behind the formation of the new Passenger Transport Executives was to create integrated transport networks through the major conurbations, initially including Liverpool, Birmingham, Newcastle – and Manchester. It was Labour Government policy, largely the brainchild of Blackburn MP Barbara Castle who was Minister of Transport in Harold Wilson's government. Ironically Manchester already had much of the benefit of through ticketing and joint services, something as we have seen it had enjoyed since Mattinson's policy in the late 1920s. Now, in a determined effort to ease congestion in the major cities, Labour wanted to go further.

The subject is far too complex for an objective view in this book, but the supposed advantage of integration with standardised vehicles and working practices came at a very high price. No one was going to willingly settle for the lowest wage or worst conditions and so operating costs and so-called 'grandfather's rights' escalated.

Meanwhile, back in Stockport, the April 1968 Transport Committee meeting authorised the invitation of tenders for ten double-deckers and by this time there was no alternative but to go for rear-engined models.

This restricted choice was quite simply because one of the schemes which the Government had created to encourage replacement of old vehicles, and to eliminate the use of conductors, was to pay a cash rebate – Bus Grant – to operators buying vehicles which conformed to its new specifications. A principal requirement was the ability to be operated by one-person. Manufacturers had a field day, order books swelled, and reliable models like the Leyland Titan, AEC Regent and Guy Arab ceased to be available.

The cost benefits – or disbenefits – can be argued at length but the yob culture of the 1990s and present day was undeniably given free reign on public transport by the removal of conductors. In many fleets passengers will not now travel upstairs because of anti-social passenger behaviour. Is this the price of so-called progress?

Three tenders were received, and these would be from Leyland, Daimler and Bristol. The Atlantean was already a byword for mechanical trouble and so, after due consideration, Bristol's tender for the VRT model was accepted. The price is not in the minutes but whilst it was not the lowest it was said to be 'the most suitable'. The price from East Lancashire Coachbuilders for the bodies at £4,655 was the lowest and was accepted.

When Stockport Corporation Transport Department duly passed to the SELNEC Passenger Transport Executive it brought to an end almost 70 years of municipal transport in the town. This was a very unpopular move locally as the Stockport undertaking was profitable and maintained its vehicles to a high standard but as has been explained the amalgamation was forced on Stockport by the Government.

No doubt the people of Stockport will have their own views, sentiment aside, as to whether or not this political move brought about an improvement in their local transport services. Sadly it will make not one jot of difference what they feel.

By early 1970 the rear-engined Bristols were complete at the works of East Lancashire Coachbuilders in Blackburn ready for delivery to Selnec but then fate took a hand when a disastrous fire occurred and all ten vehicles were destroyed, though one chassis apparently later went to Wollongong in Australia to be fitted with a locally-built body. Thus Stockport's Transport Department never did have to take the vehicles it had fought shy of, until Selnec took over and vehicle policy passed from Stockport's control.

Stockport's legacy continued, however, partly through the numbers of fine, reliable, Leyland PD2 and PD3 models it had purchased, and partly through dispersal of some of the older Leylands to SHMD and Oldham, helping out with vehicle shortages as appropriate.

And, of course, as shown at the rear of the book, several fine Stockport vehicles have survived in preservation. We can at least be thankful for that.

Standing where George Street was once the terminus of the 35C tram service, one of Stockport's handsome Leyland Titans looks rather less assured in its new colours. The lazy **S** flash, green in this case, denoted area allocations, in this case Southern, or by any other name, Stockport. Number 5853, HJA 953E, dating from 1967, had in happier days been plain number 53. Note the continued use of drop-down windows, typifying Stockport's traditional use of what it considered to be good reliable technology, whether on the body or underneath it. The 21 service was a former SHMD/Manchester joint operation to Dukinfield, Yew Tree Lane. *(STA)*

Appendix 1

TRAMCAR FLEET LIST

Year	Fleet	Type	Trucks	Body	Seating	Notes
1901	1 - 10	Double Deck Open top 4 Wheel	Brill 21E	Dick Kerr	34/20	1,3
1902	11 - 24	Double Deck Open top 4 Wheel	Brill 21E	Dick Kerr	34/22	
1903	25 - 30	Double Deck Open top 4 Wheel	Brill 21E	Dick Kerr	34/22	2
1905	31 - 40	Double Deck Open top 4 Wheel	Brill 21E	Brush	34/22	
1906	41 - 45	Double Deck Covered top 4 Wheel	Brill 21E	UEC	34/22	
1907	46 - 50	Double Deck Covered top 4 Wheel	UEC	UEC	34/22	
1919	61 - 65	Double Deck Covered top 4 Wheel	Brill 21E	English Elec./UEC	34/20	
1920	51 - 60	Double Deck Fully enclosed 4 Wheel	Brush	English Elec.	34/22	
1923	66 - 75	Double Deck Fully enclosed 4 Wheel	Craven	Craven	34/22	
1925	76 - 85	Double Deck Fully enclosed 4 Wheel	Craven	Craven	34/22	
1928	6	Double Deck Fully enclosed 4 Wheel	Brill 21E	Stockport CT	34/22	
1929	26	Double Deck Fully enclosed 4 Wheel	Craven	Stockport CT	34/22	

Notes:-
1. No. 6 was converted to a single deck salt car by 1925 and was replaced by a new No. 6 in 1928.
2. No. 26 was converted to a breakdown car in 1925 and replaced by a new No.26 in 1929.
3. No.5 is preserved in Blackpool.

Most of the cars were rebuilt and / or renumbered over the years and full details of these events can be found in the book '*Stockport Corporation Tramways*' by Maurice Marshall, published by Manchester Transport Museum Society.

Livery detail from the preserved Karrier towing wagon. *(JAS)*

Appendix 2

BUS FLEET LIST 1913 - 1969

Year	Reg.	Fleet	Chassis	Body	Notes
1913	-	1 - 3	Brush	Brush	1
1919	DB 1662-3	101-2	AEC YC	BCL & Eng. Co. B30R	
1920	DB 1814	103	AEC YC	BCL & Eng. Co. B30R	
1923	DB 3898	104	Vulcan	Vulcan B21F	
1923	DB 3897	105	Vulcan	Vulcan B21F	
1923	DB 3900	106	Vulcan	Vulcan B21F	
1923	DB 3899	107	Vulcan	Vulcan B21F	
1924	DB 5314-5	108-109	Vulcan VSD	Vulcan B26D	
1926	DB 6851	110	Leyland PLSC1	Leyland B29D	
1926	DB 6850	111	Leyland PLSC1	Leyland B29D	
1926	DB 6852-3	112-113	Leyland PLSC1	Leyland B29D	
1926	DB 7460-5	114-119	Leyland PLSC1	Leyland B29D	
1927	DB 8396-8	120-122	Leyland PLSC1	Short B34D	
1928	DB 9157-68	123-134	Leyland PLSC1	Cravens B32D	
1929	JA 377-88	135-146	AEC Reliance	Cravens B32D	
1930	JA 1027-32	147-152	AEC Reliance	Cravens B30D	
1930	JA 1291	153	AEC Regent	Short H24/26R	2
1930	JA 1465-70	159-164	Leyland TS3	Leyland B30D	
1931	JA 1459-64	153-158	Crossley Alpha	Crossley B32D	
1934	JA 5442-3	165-166	Leyland TD3	Leyland H26/26R	
1935	JA 6213-6	167-170	Leyland TD4c	Leyland H28/24R	
1936	JA 7571-8	171-178	Leyland TD4c	Leyland H28/24R	
1936	JA 7583-92	183-192	Leyland TS7	English Electric B35C	
1937	JA 7579-82	179-182	Leyland TD4c	Leyland H28/24R	
1937	JA 7593-602	193-202	Leyland TS8	English Electric B35C	
1940	JA 7604	204	Leyland TD7	Leyland H30/26R	
1940	JA 7606	206	Leyland TD7	Leyland H30/26R	
1940	JA 7608	208	Leyland TD7	Leyland H30/26R	
1941	JA 7603	203	Crossley Mancunian	Crossley H30/26R	
1941	JA 7605	205	Crossley Mancunian	Crossley H30/26R	
1943	JA 7609-10	209-210	Guy Arab 2	Massey H30/26R	
1944	JA 7611-18	211-218	Guy Arab 2	Massey H30/26R	
1945	JA 7619-24	219-224	Guy Arab 2	Massey H30/26R	
1946	JA 7607	207	Crossley DD42/3	Crossley H30/26R	
1946	JA 7625-30	225-230	Crossley DD24/3	Crossley H30/26R	
1946	CDB 1-10	231-240	Crossley DD42/3	Crossley H30/26R	
1947	CDB 11-14	241-244	Crossley DD42/3	Crossley H30/26R	

Year	Reg.	Fleet	Chassis	Body	Notes
1948	CJA 769-78	245-254	Crossley DD42/5	Crossley H30/26R	
1948	CJA 779-88	255-264	Crossley DD42/5	Crossley H30/26R	
1949	DJA 173-85	265-277	Leyland PD2/1	Leyland H30/26R	
1949	DJA 186-92	278-284	Leyland PD2/1	Leyland H30/26R	
1951	EDB 539-62	285-308	Leyland PD2/1	Leyland H30/26R	
1951	EDB 563-86	309-332	Crossley DD42/7	Crossley H30/26R	
1958	NDB 353-5	333-5	Leyland PSUC1/1	Crossley B44F	3
1958	NDB 360-5	337-342	Leyland PD2/30	Crossley H33/28R	
1958	NDB 366-369	343-6	Leyland PD2/30	Crossley H33/28R	4
1958	NDB 356	403	Leyland PSUC1/1	Crossley B44F	
1960	PJA 913-22	343-352	Leyland PD2/30	Longwell Gn. H32/28R	
1962	VDB 584-93	353-362	Leyland PD2A/30	East Lancs H32/28R	
1963	YDB 1-10	1 - 10	Leyland PD2A/30	East Lancs H36/28R	
1964	BJA 911-25B	11-25	Leyland PD2/40	East Lancs H36/28R	
1965	FDB 326-40C	26-40	Leyland PD2/40	East Lancs H36/28R	
1967	HJA 941-55E	41-55	Leyland PD2/40	East Lancs H36/28R	
1967	HJA 956-70E	56-70	Leyland PD2/40	Neepsend H36/28R	5
1968	KJA 871-85F	71-85	Leyland PD3/14	East Lancs H38/32R	
1968	KDB 404-08F	404-408	Leyland PSU4/1R	East Lancs B43D	
1969	MJA 886-91G	86-91	Leyland PD3/14	East Lancs H38/32R	
1969	MJA 892-97G	92-97	Leyland PD3/14	East Lancs H38/32F	

Notes :-
1. Trolleybuses
2. Vehicle on loan
3. 333-5 were renumbered 400-2 shortly after entering service
4. 343-6 were renumbered 333-6 shortly after entering service
5. Neepsend Coachworks was an associated company of East Lancashire Coachbuilders and built bodies to East Lancs designs
   A batch of 10 Bristol VRTSL6G double-deckers with East Lancs bodies was ordered in 1969 but was destroyed in the fire at East Lancs works at Easter 1970

Abbreviations
1. BCL & Eng. Co - British Commercial Lorry and Engineering

PJA 918, formerly number 348, became a driver trainer as seen here, and was numbered TV.1. Such vehicles were retained by virtue of their non-automatic gearboxes, as drivers passed on automatics were restricted to driving vehicles with that type of transmission. *(STA)*

Appendix 3

COMMENCEMENT DATES FOR BUS SERVICES 1913 - 1951

Date	Route No.	Route	Notes
10.03.1913		Stockport - Offerton	Trolleybus service
08.10.1919		Stockport - Offerton	Petrol bus service
14.03.1927	(16)	Stockport - Heaton Mersey	
09.09.1928	(16)	Stockport - Kingsway	
06.10.1929	(16)	Stepping Hill - West Didsbury	
18.02.1946	16	Stepping Hill - Chorlton	
09.03.1923	(9)	Reddish - Green Lane	
09.05.1923	(9)	Reddish - Heaton Mersey	
06.10.1929	(9)	Reddish - West Didsbury	
09.01.1928	(47)	Cheadle Heath - Crossley Road	
30.01.1928	(29)	Stockport - Hyde	
20.09.1930	30/31	Stockport - Hyde - Ashton / Stalybridge	
02.03.1947	29	Stockport - Hyde	Buses replaced trams
04.05.1947	29	Stockport - Bredbury	
04.03.1951	30/31	Edgeley - Ashton	Buses replaced trams
04.03.1951	30/31	Edgeley - Vernon Park	Buses replaced trams
29.09.1928	(23)	Stockport - Woodsmoor	
05.07.1931	23		Service extended to Egerton Road.
05.02.1933	23		Resumed running to Woodsmoor Lane / Bramhall Lane
09.06.1946	23		Service extended to Crossway
12.10.1930	24	Stockport - Adswood via Shaw Heath	
14.12.1930	24	Stockport - Adswood via Edgeley	
15.02.1931			Service terminated at Stockholm Road
22.02.1931			Service withdrawn
09.08.1948	25	Stockport - Adswood via Davenport	
28.12.1930	40	Stockport - Gatley	
28.02.1949	40		Service extended to Stonepail Road
04.03.1951	39		Additional service to Councillor Lane Tramways withdrawn
07.01.1929		Dialstone Lane - Hollinwood	
15.05.1929			Service terminated at Manchester
25.11.1929		Dialstone Lane - Worsley	
20.03.1933			Service terminated at Manchester
15.02.1932	20	Manchester - Poynton	Poynton Church
10.08.1934	20		Service extended to Lostock Road
06.08.1936	20A	Manchester - Woodford	Service taken over from J Sharp
13.06.1932		Stockport - Woodbank - Hempshaw La. - Cheadle Heath	
23.04.1933		Stockport - Lowndes Lane	
26.07.1937	75	Green End - Offerton	
11.07.1949		Stockport - Mirrlees Works	
01.05.1930		Reddish - Manchester, Lwr Mosley St	
19.10.1930		Andrew Square - Manchester, Lwr Mosley St	
29.10.1930	74	Vernon Park - Manchester, Lwr Mosley St	
08.11.1931	74	Vernon Park - Manchester, Parker Street	
09.04.1933	33	Romiley - Manchester, Parker Street	
17.05.1934	33	Greave - Manchester, Parker Street	
23.05.1938	33	Andrew Square - Manchester, Parker Street	
11.10.1936	74	Manchester - Cheadle - Stockport	
04.03.1951	74		Service extended to St Pauls, Portwood
16.02.1948	89	St. Peters Square - Manchester, Albert Sq	Tramways withdrawn
10.01.1949	92	Hazel Grove - Manchester, Piccadilly	Tramways withdrawn
19.12.1927		Dialstone Lane - Bury	
20.03.1933			Service terminated at Manchester
12.08.1951	17	Stockport - Reddish	Tramways withdrawn

Appendix 4

SCHEDULE OF TRAM AND BUS SERVICES AS AT 1938

Route	Details	Joint Operators
Bus Services		
6	West Didsbury - Stockport - Stepping Hill	
9	West Didsbury - Heaton Moor - Reddish	
16	Stepping Hill - Stockport - Heaton Mersey - Parrs Wood	MCT
18	Manchester, Parker Street - Stockport, Dialstone Lane	MCT
20	Manchester, Parker Street - Stockport - Poynton	MCT
20A	Manchester, Parker Street - Stockport - Woodford	MCT, NWRC
23	Stockport - Woodsmoor	
24	Stockport - Adswood (Garners Lane)	
26	Stockport - Mile End	
27	Stockport - Bredbury via New Zealand Road	
29	Stockport - Bredbury - Woodley - Hyde	SHMD
30	Stockport - Bredbury - Woodley - Hyde - Stalybridge	SHMD
31	Stockport - Hyde - Ashton	ACT. SHMD
33	Manchester, Parker Street - Stockport - Romiley/Greave	MCT, NWRC
33X	Manchester, Parker Street - Stockport (Andrew Square)	MCT
37	Stockport - Heaton Chapel (Crossley Road)	
38	Stockport - Edgeley - Cheadle (Councillor Lane)	
39	Parrs Wood - Kingsway - Mersey Square - Reddish	
40	Stockport - Cheadle - Gatley	
47	Cheadle (Councillor Lane) - Stockport - Heaton Chapel (Crossley Road)	
56	Stockport - Offerton - Hempshaw Lane - Cheadle	
74	Manchester, Parker Street - Parrs Wood - Cheadle - Stockport, Mersey Square	MCT
75	Offerton - Stockport - Green End	
Tram Services		
1	Reddish - Stockport - Cheadle Heath	
2	Edgeley - Dale Street - Stockport - Hyde	SHMD
2A	Edgeley - Dale Street - Stockport - Bredbury Bar	
2B	Edgeley - Dale Street - Bents Lane	
3	Reddish - Stockport - Hazel Grove	
4A	Stockport St Peter's Square - Hazel Grove	
33	Manchester - Belle Vue - Reddish, Vale Road	MCT
35	Manchester, Exchange - Stockport - Hazel Grove	MCT
35A	Manchester, Exchange - Stockport, Mersey Square	MCT
35B	Manchester, Albert Square - Stockport, St. Peter's Square	MCT
35C	Manchester, Piccadilly - Stockport, St. Peter's Square	MCT

Key to Other Operators

ACT	Ashton Corporation Transport
MCT	Manchester Corporation Transport
SHMD	Stalybridge, Hyde, Mossley and Dukinfield Joint Transport Undertaking
NWRC	North Western Road Car Company Ltd

Appendix 5

SCHEDULE OF BUS SERVICES AS AT 1963

Route	Details	Vehicle numbers of Joint Operators
9	West Didsbury – Heaton Moor – Reddish	
16	Stepping Hill – Stockport – Heaton Mersey – Chorlton	SCT 4; MCT 2
17	Stockport – Reddish	
17X	Reddish – Stockport – Hazel Grove	
18	Bramhall Moor Lane – Manchester, Chorlton Street	SCT 3; MCT 2
20/20A	Poynton/Woodford – Stockport – Manchester, Chorlton Street	SCT 2; MCT 3; NWRCC 3
22	Stockport – Adswood, Bridge Hall Road	
23	Stockport – Woodsmoor	
24	Stockport – Adswood, Garners Lane	
25	Stockport – Davenport Station – Adswood, Garners Lane	
26	Mile End Lane – Stockport – Heaton Mersey - Parr's Wood	
27	Stockport – New Zealand Road – Bredbury	
29/29A	Edgeley – Stockport – Bredbury – Woodley – Hyde	SCT 5; SHMD 3
30/31	Edgeley – Stockport – Bredbury – Woodley – Hyde – Ashton	SCT 5; SHMD 4; ACT 3
33	Greave – Romiley – Stockport – Manchester, Chorlton Street	SCT 2; MCT 2; NWRCC 0
33X	Andrew Square – Stockport – Manchester, Chorlton Street	SCT 2; MCT 2
38	Stockport – Woodbank Estate	
39	Stockport – Cheadle Heath – Cheadle, Councillor Lane	
40	Stockport – Cheadle – Gatley	
47	Heaton Chapel – Stockport – Edgeley – Cheadle, Councillor Lane	
55/56/81A	Stockport – Brinnington	SCT 4; NWRCC 4
74	Portwood – Cheadle – Manchester, Chorlton Street	SCT 4; MCT 4
75	Offerton – Stockport – Green End	
89	St Peter's Square – Stockport – Manchester, Albert Square	SCT 2; MCT 4
90	Marple – Romiley – Bredbury – Hyde – Stalybridge	SCT 0; SHMD 2; NWRCC 2
92	Hazel Grove – Stockport – Manchester, Piccadilly	SCT 9; MCT 8

Key to Joint Operators

ACT – Ashton-under-Lyne Corporation Transport;   NWRCC – North Western Road Car Company

MCT – Manchester Corporation Transport;   SHMD – Stalybridge, Hyde, Mossley & Dukinfield Jt Bd

Before the arrival of Selnec upset the applecart, scenes such as this, with
Stockport and Ashton vehicles in this instance, were commonplace. *(STA)*

Appendix 6

JOINT OPERATION

As has been seen on the previous page Stockport, like all the twelve municipal operators in the Manchester area, had joint routes with its neighbours. Inevitably, the majority of these were operated with Manchester. In the upper picture in Piccadilly, 1951 Leyland PD2 No. 308 (which is now preserved) is about to depart to Dialstone Lane, Stockport on service 18, whilst alongside is Manchester Corporation No. 3326, another PD2 but with a body by Northern Counties of Wigan. Service 74 took the long way round via Cheadle and Parrs Wood to Stockport, terminating at Vernon Park. Both these services were jointly operated. In the lower picture in Mersey Square, Manchester Corporation Burlingham-bodied Leyland PD2 number 3489 is about to depart for Chorlton, also via Parrs Wood on joint service 16, having arrived from Dialstone Lane. Note that the 24 loading at the parallel stand is going in the opposite direction – this could cause chaos for passengers at peak periods. *(NDC; STA)*

Appendix 7

MEMORIES of MERSEY SQUARE

by Cliff Marsh

To a very young teenager who, in the early nineteen fifties, was rapidly developing an interest in all forms of road transport, but particularly buses, there were two what I would today describe as 'centres of excellence' which I became aware of, where the bus scene could be observed.

One was the famous Coliseum Bus Station in Blackpool, where company-operated coaches and buses from all over Lancashire and Yorkshire as well as further afield, could be found. Often there was also a smattering of Corporation and independent operators' vehicles hired in by such companies as North Western Road Car Co Ltd to cope with the massive influx of holidaymakers journeying to and from the town. These would be needed particularly during Wakes Week holiday periods, when northern industrial towns shut down for annual holidays.

The second, and more important to me because it was local and visited two or three times a week, was Mersey Square in the centre of Stockport, and the focus for bus operation in the town. Here there could be seen over the years a mixed array of vehicles, both company and municipal. The municipal operators passing through the square included vehicles in the blue and cream livery of Ashton under Lyne Corporation, and the green and cream of the Stalybridge, Hyde, Mossley and Dukinfield Joint Transport and Electricity Undertaking (SHMD), as well as the red and cream liveries of Manchester and Stockport Corporations. The square was also the centre for North Western services starting from the town, and a mixed bag of their red and cream vehicles could be found, along with occasional vehicles from Ribble and Trent on jointly operated express services. Quite frequently vehicles also appeared from North Western's subsidiary fleets of Melba Motors and Altrincham Coachways, whilst on a Saturday morning in holiday periods what seemed like dozens of AEC Regals of the Midland General and Mansfield District fleets would come racing down the A6 alongside the Square to climb up Wellington Road *en route* probably to Blackpool via Manchester.

The mixture of vehicles observed, over a relatively brief number of years, was equally fascinating. The Stockport fleet included Massey-bodied utility Guy Arabs as well as prewar and postwar Leylands and Crossleys, the latter built a few miles north of the Square at the Erwood Park factory on the Manchester boundary. The prewar Titans were Leyland-bodied as were the early postwar vehicles, but later deliveries would include Titans bodied by Crossley, Longwell Green and East Lancashire. The prewar Tigers had centre entrance bodies by English Electric, with postwar Tiger Cubs bodied by Crossley. SHMD double-deckers (occasionally their rare Northern Counties-bodied Atkinson one) and Ashton under Lyne Titans would be jointly working with Stockport Corporation from Edgeley west of the town, through the Square and out to Hyde and Ashton.

The North Western fleet in the early to mid nineteen fifties was incredibly varied, a result at least in part of the company becoming part of the BET empire, this eventually preventing the purchase of ECW-bodied Bristol vehicles. Occasionally the last of the Dennis Lancets could be seen at the start of the decade, along with Bristol Ls, Ks, Leyland Tigers and Guy Arabs rebodied in the post-war period. Also at the start of the decade, the last of the Bristol Ls which could be purchased were in evidence, along with Windover-bodied coaches on both Bristol L and Leyland chassis delivered in 1949/50. The latter had caused me some concern until I realised the Leyland chassis were a mixture of rebodied pre-war TS8 chassis and new PS2 chassis. Thus I became aware of the difference between pre-war and post-war Leyland radiators. To me 1952 to 1954 were vintage years, Atkinson single-deckers with Weymann bodies, Leyland Royal Tigers with magnificent Leyland coach and Weymann bus bodies, two Leyland Olympics and the first Tiger Cubs with both bus and coach bodies all arrived on the scene along with the first AEC Reliances. On the double-deck scene, Leyland PD1As with ECW bodies were already in evidence, joined by PD2s carrying a mixture of Leyland and Weymann bodies. I particularly remember the end of the decade travelling from Stockport on the Olympics which often appeared on the 27 Buxton to Manchester Lower Moseley Street service. Although well into their working life by that time, they seemed to have an incredible turn of speed and as they climbed out of Mersey Square up the hill on the A6 they always seemed able to overtake early postwar cars with ease. I am convinced, however, that even with local inhabitants of the area the indicators on these and other North Western vehicles would appear confusing, as they read 'Manchester LMS', many thinking this was a railway station and not Lower Moseley Street Bus Station, itself another fascinating centre of bus operation. Over a relatively short period of years the variety of bus bodies to be found was also incredible and included examples by Weymann, Leyland, ECW, Crossley, Bond, Willowbrook, Massey, Brush, English Electric, Burlingham, Northern Counties and Windover.

The most memorable and probably busiest times in the Square were late Friday afternoons. The Square would be seething with activity, a combination of shoppers and workers going home, many of the latter having journeyed into the Square from one side of the town, possibly on a workers' service, to catch a bus passing through or starting from the Square to some surrounding district. To understand the chaos which could occur certainly in parts of the Square, the layout of the buildings surrounding it must be appreciated. One one side of the Square opposite the A6 were the old tram shed and the fire station

side by side   The tram shed housed buses as well as a decreasing number of trams and was set back approximately two bus lengths from the Square itself. In the middle of the entrance area to the shed, and at right angles to the Square, was an enclosed passenger shelter. Buses heading to the Offerton and Stepping Hill parts of the town loaded here. There was room either side of the shelter for buses or trams to enter or exit the shed, as well as fire engines returning via the side entrance into the fire station. For me, waiting in the shelter was fascinating. I would have the choice of three services home and the anticipation was in weighing up which service and therefore which vehicle would arrive first or whether a number would all arrive together. The 16 service from Chorlton to Stepping Hill via Mersey Square was jointly operated by Manchester and Stockport Corporations and was served over the years by prewar Manchester Leyland Titans (streamliners) and later postwar PD2s from Parrs Wood garage. Stockport would provide either a new all-Leyland PD2 or a Crossley-bodied Crossley. However, there were also short workings of the 16 route (route 26) operated by Stockport and starting from the Square. At rush hours additional workings or duplicates would be provided. Vehicles required could be seen pulling out of the bus garage on the corner of the Square waiting at the traffic lights to cross the A6 into the Square to take up their rota. These could include prewar Leyland-bodied Titans, Crossleys or Massey-bodied utility Guy Arabs. Often this would coincide with a bus arriving on route 16 from Chorlton. Thus, suddenly a number of buses would arrive at the shelter together. In addition a bus returning from Offerton may well arrive to take up

In the period following the closure of the tramway system (1951) and the building of the Merseyway Shopping Precinct (1967), only one area of the Square was modified to any extent, with bus stops and termini of that period located as on the map. The modified section was that parallel to the A6 between the Bear Pit and Princes Street which previously had allowed bus and tram access along its length in and out of the Square. This area was now pedestrianised to provide sites for bus stops for routes heading south along the A6 and more space for routes terminating in the Square itself.

Bus Routes

A 17 Reddish
B 18,92 towards Hazel Grove, (joint MCT, SCT)
C As B, but towards Manchester
D 16 towards Chorlton (joint MCT, SCT); 26 towards Parrs Wood; 75 towards Green End; 22,23,24,25 to Adswood, Davenport, Woodsmoor; 27 Bredbury
E 16 towards Stepping Hill (joint MCT, SCT); 26,36,38,75 towards Offerton
F All NWRC services (including 81A joint with SCT)
G 29,30,31 towards Hyde, Ashton (joint SHMD, AuL, SCT); 74 towards Portwood (joint MCT, SCT)
H As G, but towards Edgeley; 74 towards Manchester (joint MCT, SCT)
J 37,39,40 to Cheadle, Gatley

Just as I was trying to find one picture to sum up the whole scene Bob Rowe produced this marvellous shot taken during his time with North Western. Notice the crowds of people waiting to take the bus after work finished – the age of the motor car in nearly every family home has yet to make an impact here. Prior to the development of the M60 Mersey Square was a crossing point for east-west and north-south traffic, hence the road sign in centre left of the picture. A feature at night was the Inspector's whistle signifying the departure of the last buses for the day. (RGR)

its place with the others already lined up.

On a wet miserable Friday afternoon, four or five buses double-parked could be outside the shelter. The queue of passengers and waiting buses would extend beyond the shelter itself and across the front of the fire station. Then of course, the inevitable would happen, the alarm would sound and the emerging appliances would scatter the passengers forcing any buses blocking the exit to take a trip around the Square. Not a situation which would be tolerated today contravening Health and Safety requirements but a fascinating one for a young bus enthusiast who, by now, had made his way through the chaos between the vehicles, taking in the smell of hot oil and exhaust fumes, to board a utility Massey-bodied Guy Arab complete with wooden seats, vibrating body and throbbing Gardner engine.

As the years rolled on, other routes were added to the Offerton area to cope with extending housing estates. However, mention must be made of the third long-standing route to the area, the 75 service. This was a service always operated by English Electric centre entrance bodied prewar Leyland Tigers. To me this was the nearest one could get to a country bus route operating in suburbia. The service always seemed to be operated by the same crews, so much so that vehicles would halt between stops without being requested to do so to set down almost adjacent to their homes elderly ladies carrying numerous bags full of the week's shopping from the market. It was easy to miss the Tigers, they would pull up alongside the double-deckers, making it difficult for them to be seen and only the 'regulars' seemed familiar with their arrival. Once full, the manual sliding door would be closed and when the guard had completed his duties he would stand on the saloon steps to operate the door, chatting to passengers whilst often smoking a 'Woodbine'. The atmosphere on the bus, with door and all windows closed, a full load of passengers, many of them smoking on a wet day is an unforgettable memory. The TS7s and TS8s were replaced in 1958 by Crossley-bodied Leyland Tiger Cubs and on a number of occasions, I recall unscheduled stops outside the driver's house to allow his wife to give him his billycan with fresh brew, to be consumed at the Offerton terminus. I often wondered if it would be shared with the guard.

The other potentially chaotic area in the Square was the southern corner. This was where most of the North Western services started from, intermingling

Exactly as I remember it, with a steady stream of traffic in Merseyway filtering into the Square. Close inspection reveals an SHMD Brush-bodied Daimler at the kerbside bus stop, *en route* to Edgeley. Behind the Corporation Crossley one of North Western's Willowbrook-bodied lowbridge double-deckers is almost hidden. Ford's Consul 375, an Austin A35 van and a Hillman Minx saloon are to the fore with a prewar Austin having just been overtaken by the Champion bread van. On the right hand edge of the picture a Leyland-bodied Leyland PD2 from the North Western fleet awaits the signal to proceed. *(CMC)*

with those of the Corporation. The chaos would occur as both Corporation and North Western vehicles, often moving in opposite directions, sought access to adjacent passenger stands. In addition, an area outside the North Western office would accommodate buses parked behind each other and often three abreast, the rear vehicles actually turning round in part of the road that went underneath the A6 road. This was one of two roads with a public house separating them, which allowed North Western buses access to an area of waste ground where they could park. In later years, this became the bus station. Family outings on a Saturday afternoon often ended with 'afternoon tea' in the second floor restaurant of the Plaza Cinema which overlooked the Square, giving a wonderful view of all the bus movements. Many of the vehicles had to cross from one side of the Square to the other, seeking exits to virtually all points of the compass. Eventually, a roundabout was constructed in the middle, resulting in a log jam at busy times of buses and other vehicles endeavouring to exit in their chosen direction. Looking back, however, I cannot recall any serious accidents occurring in the Square, despite the crowds of people and mix of vehicles using it. The worst I recall was of a cyclist becoming stuck in the tram tracks, the trams still being in use in the Square until 1951 and adding further to the chaos. This part of the Square also had Corporation vehicles passing through it, plus North Western vehicles on the 28 Manchester to Hayfield route operated by rebodied prewar Bristol K5Gs, some of which remained in service until 1965, together with vehicles on the 27 Manchester to Buxton route. The latter route was operated by an assortment of vehicles over the years including the aforementioned Olympics, Atkinsons, Tiger Cubs and Royal Tigers as well as prewar and postwar Bristol L5Gs and demonstration vehicles. North Western express services including the X2 Manchester to Nottingham service also stopped in the Square.

Having been actively concerned with preservation, for more years than I care to remember, I do regret not being able to become involved earlier when it may have been possible to preserve a Massey-bodied utility Guy Arab or one of the prewar all-Leyland Titans, some of which survived until the early 'sixties. However, a good number of Stockport vehicles have survived, particularly Leyland PD2s and PD3s, and I am thankful to have been able to play a part in securing a number of them together with a Crossley-bodied Crossley, important as a vehicle in its own right, and also representing part of the town's industrial history.

Manchester had its Piccadilly and Lower Moseley Street bus stations, Liverpool its Pier Head and I know there were many other centres up and down the country of equal interest. However, if the then fledgling *'Buses Illustrated'* could have conducted a nationwide popularity poll of the best bus spotting centres, I think Mersey Square, Stockport, would have been near the top. Certainly it would for me.

North Western Alexander-bodied Daimler Fleetlines stand by the Mersey Square office. *(RGR)*

Appendix 8

TICKETS

from Brian Hughes collection

DETAILS OF TICKETS SHOWN OPPOSITE

1. Child to/from school, morning or afternoon
2. As above with spaces for TRANSFER at top
3. Shorter ticket with value lower down
4. Four stages only, no transfer facilities
5. Composite – single or return – no transfer
6. Composite – facility for two transfers
7. Composite – all tickets over 6d had the red line
8. Co-ordinated motor bus ticket from Stockport, each operator showed their own title
9. Issued to passengers travelling before 9am, with their own ticket, for return on day of issue only
10. Ticket for ROF factory Risley
11. Roll ticket for Lyme Park service
12. Spitfire Fund ticket/receipt
13. TIM ticket used after Bell Punch discontinued; either machine is new or has just been converted to issue tickets in decimal currency

The Bell Punch type of ticket, as seen below, could be found all over Great Britain. Each ticket carried a number and value and numbers for the stages along the route for which it was valid. The conductor had a cash bag over one shoulder, and the cancelling punch over the other, and would take a ticket (or tickets if more than one was needed to cover the value of the journey) and punch them in the punch shown alongside the ticket rack. This punch gave a loud TING which confirmed to all and sundry that the ticket had been punched, and a small hole appeared in the ticket to show where the passenger had boarded. Inspectors could thus easily check if a passenger was attempting to ride beyond his or her stop. The punchings were retained inside the punch and could be counted – including checking the colours! – to verify the number issued in cases where the numbers of tickets issued did not tally with the conductor's takings. The TIM machine, also below, was a mobile printing unit which used blank rolls of paper as shown, and printed all the required details from information dialed in by the conductor. It also held a record of the number and value of tickets issued, whilst the paper rolls were of virtually no value whereas stolen tickets could be sold at face value. *(Below and facing: Tickets etc Brian Hughes, photography JAS)*

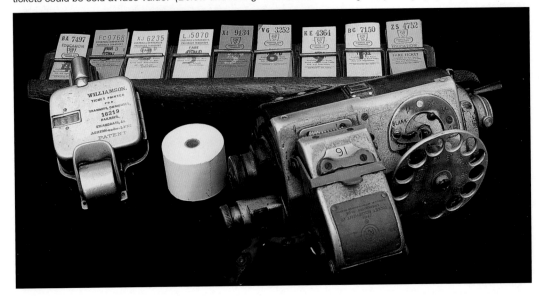

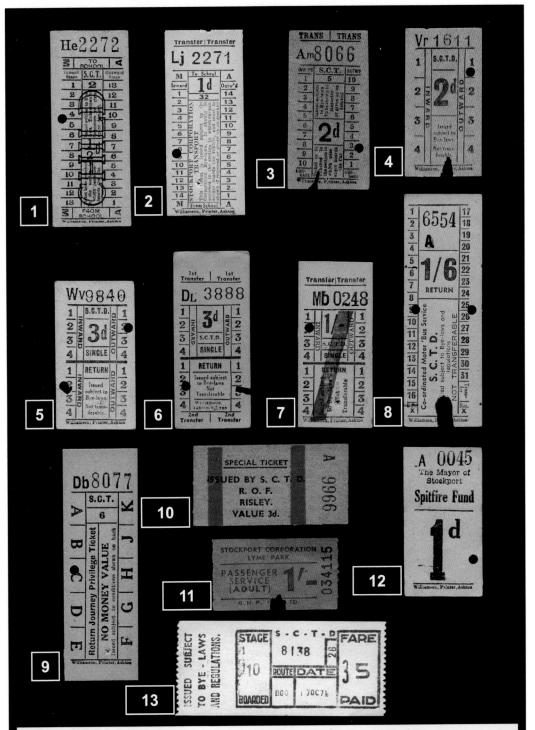

Stockport followed the usual path in regard to ticketing, and we are fortunate in being able to illustrate a selection of the Bell Punch tickets used on the buses and trams, together with an example of the TIM roll which followed the Bell Punch. We are also extremely fortunate in being able to show the method of fare collection – without tickets – used on the horse trams before the Corporation took over responsibility for transport in the Borough. The Kaye's Patent Fare Box features a glass top, with slot, through which the passenger drops his or her fare. One survives at Heaton Park and was brought out of retirement as shown when the Eades reversible tram was launched in April 2008. *(MTMS; JAS)*

Facing page: The maroon flash was a distinctive feature of the English Electric-bodied Leylands which were clearly influenced by body styling developed for Ribble Motor Services, and all of which had a long life. This was partly due to the presence of a very low bridge by the Bird Hall trading estate which these vehicles frequented through various works services. Number 192 is seen in Mersey Square, 200 outside Heaton Lane depot, and the former 185 after conversion to working for Social Services including gaining wheel trims. In their original use these vehicles also worked an internal service in Lyme Park, taking visitors from the gates to the Hall up the long driveway (see tickets page). The view above demonstrates only too clearly the difficulty in adapting a former tram depot, in this case Mersey Square, for bus work. The narrow doorways, awkwardly placed columns and internal pillars made parking and manoeuvring very difficult. Following the withdrawals of the Tigers, Social Services acquired two former Huddersfield Corporation Guy UF single-deckers, FVH 1/2, with bodywork also by Guy. They perpetuated the use of the names Endeavour 1 and 2. *(Facing and above, NDC all. Below, STA)*

Advertising on Stockport's buses must have been relatively cheap if a small specialist shop could afford to use the facility. EDB 542 is heading for Edgeley on the joint Ashton, SHMD, Stockport service. *(GL)*

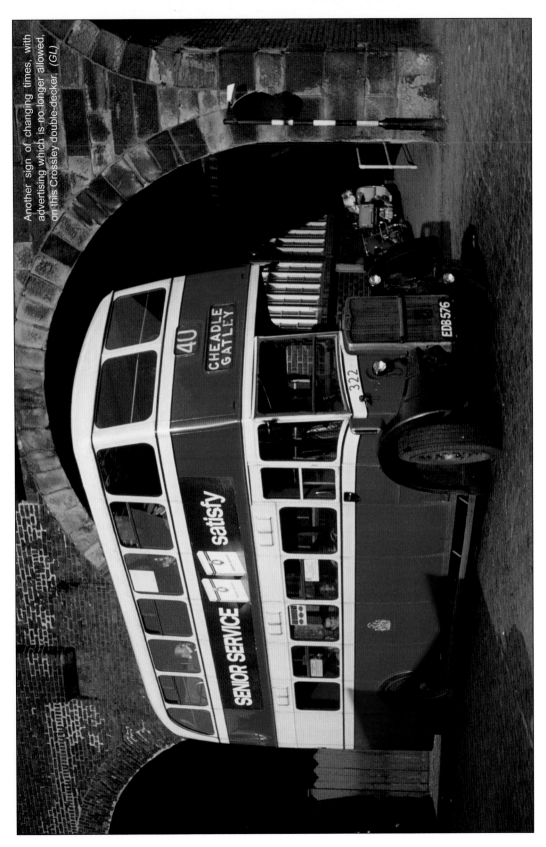

Another sign of changing times, with advertising which is no longer allowed, on this Crossley double-decker. (GL)

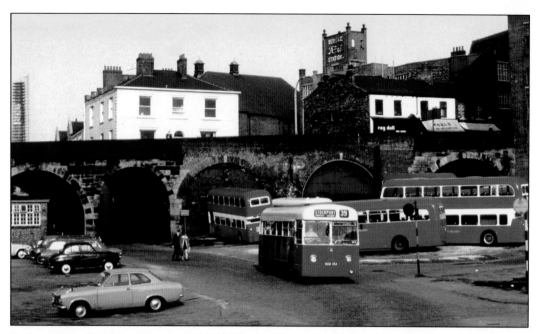

On the western side of the A6, where the bus station now stands, Crossley-bodied Leyland Tiger Cub 408 heads out to Councillor Lane on the 39 service, despite what the blind says. In the background a selection of North Western vehicles can be seen, including two of the Daimler Fleetlines which Stockport had eschewed in favour of the Bristol VRs it never got. On the extreme left the brick building has now become North Western's crew room. Had the photographer been standing further back more North Western vehicles would have been in view in an area where perhaps 30 or more buses could be parked up between duties. *(CMC)*

Three faces of Leyland PD2s with traditional and concealed radiators. Below, number 8 of the batch 1-10 of 1963 carries the St Helens style front, whilst on the facing page number 54, above, has the traditional exposed radiator, The Longwell Green-bodied example, below, PJA 914, ex 344 and now 5944, is leaving the Norfolk Arms in Glossop, working the Glossop to Manchester number 6 service, one in which Stockport had no interest until its vehicles passed to the PTE after January 1969. This bus would then have been transferred as part of the general move round. Other former Stockport Leylands went to the SHMD area. *(GL two, JAS)*

STOCKPORT CORPORATION TRANSPORT DEPARTMENT

CHANGE OF ADDRESS

Will you kindly note that from

15th JANUARY, 1968

our new address will be:—

DAW BANK, STOCKPORT

Phone: **STOckport 4001** (5 lines)

Appendix 10

LIST OF PRESERVED VEHICLES

Year	Reg.	Fleet	Chassis	Body	Owner	Notes
1926	YM 9410	106	Karrier	Tower Wagon	MOT, Manchester	
1938	ADB 353		Dennis Ajax	Tower Wagon	N.McQueen, Durham	1
1935/6	JA 7585	185	Leyland TS7	English Electric B35C	MOT, Manchester	2
1935/6	JA 7591	191	Leyland TS7	English Electric B35C	D. Hoare, Chepstow	3
1951	EDB 549	295	Leyland PD2/1	Leyland OH30/26R	MOT, Manchester	4
1951	EDB 562	308	Leyland PD2/1	Leyland H30/26R	MOT, Manchester	
1951	EDB 575	321	Crossley DD42	Crossley H30/26R	MOT, Manchester	5
1958	NDB 356	403	Leyland PSUC1/1	Crossley B44F	QMS	6
1968	KDB 408F	408	Leyland PSU4/1	East Lancs. B43D	M Prescott	
1965	FDB 328C	28	Leyland PD2/40	East Lancs. H36/28R	BBPG	
1965	FDB 331C	31	Leyland PD2/40	East Lancs. H36/28R	Gowdy, Ballyclare	
1965	FDB 334C	34	Leyland PD2/40	East Lancs. H36/28R	R Steele, Crewe	
1965	FDB 340C	40	Leyland PD2/40	East Lancs. H36/28R	Wheels (A Wakelin)	
1967	HJA 952E	52	Leyland PD2/40	East Lancs. H36/28R	G & W, Crewe	
1967	HJA 965E	65	Leyland PD2/40	Neepsend H36/28R	QMS	
1968	KJA 871F	71	Leyland PD3/14	East Lancs. H38/36R	MOT, Manchester	7
1969	MJA 888G	88	Leyland PD3/14	East Lancs. H38/32R	Johnson et al Northwich	
1969	MJA 891G	91	Leyland PD3/14	East Lancs. H38/32R	MOT, Manchester	8
1969	MJA 893G	93	Leyland PD3/14	East Lancs. H38/32F	Finch, Higher Ince	
1969	MJA 895G	95	Leyland PD3/14	East Lancs. H38/32F	BBPG	
1969	MJA 897G	97	Leyland PD3/14	East Lancs. OH38/32F	MOT, Manchester	9

Abbreviations :-

MOT	Museum of Transport, Boyle Street Manchester.
QMS	Quantock Motor Services.
BBPG	British Bus Preservation Group.
G&W Crewe	Garside & Whitaker, Crewe.

Notes :-

1. Usually ran with trade plate 161 DB
2. Used by Stockport Social Services, painted green and cream, fitted with rear wheelchair lift, named 'Endeavour 1'
3. As 2 named 'Endeavour 2' wheelchair lift removed
4. Used by SCT as a tree lopper, replacing Crossley JA 7626
5. Formerly with SELNEC Transport Society
6. One of the last Crossley bodies built
7. Restored in SELNEC livery fleet number 5871
8. Last rear entrance open platform bus to enter service in Great Britain
9. Restored in Museum of Transport, Manchester livery, as an open-topper

> Facing page: One of the select band of preserved tramcars which have operated over the Blackpool system's tracks is Stockport's number 5. After withdrawal the lower saloon was used a bird watchers' hut for many years before it was rescued from its Derbyshire home and, over a long period, and in several locations, was restored to full working order, going to Blackpool in 1996. Its Brill truck came from Portugal. *(RF)*

This neat Dennis Ajax tower wagon is now preserved in County Durham. It joined the fleet in 1938 and was sold for preservation after being withdrawn. In addition to its obvious appurtenances it was fitted with a bicycle wheel attachment with a mileometer attachment which could be trailed behind for measuring route distances. After the new Daw Bank facility was opened in 1968, a selection of vehicles was later assembled and posed for photography as seen below. Nearest the camera is one of the instantly recognisable centre-entrance English Electric-bodied Leyland Tigers, JA 7585, number 185. On the facing page can be seen the other survivor, No. 191, and also the sole survivor of Stockport's Crossley fleet, double-decker 321 from 1951, which had just had its second overhaul and repaint in preservation and positively gleamed when it was photographed at Astley Green colliery, starting point for the annual August Trans-Pennine run to Harrogate, which in earlier days left from Belle Vue, Manchester. The front destination blind – fitted by Maurice Marshall – was formerly in one of the Mancunians, Nos. 203/5, and accordingly includes destinations such as New Mills which were part of a proposed reorganisation and pooling of services with North Western in 1938. The scheme was dropped, partly because of the imminent likelihood of World War 2. Maurice quite clearly did not set the blind display on this occasion. *(CMC two; JAS; NDC opposite)*

Two of the six Stockport preserved Leyland Titans are seen here, number 34 a PD2 and number 91, a 30ft-long PD3, the last rear entrance open platform double-decker to enter service in Britain. Both are bodied by East Lancashire Coachbuilders of Blackburn and there can be no denying that this must be one of the best-ever designs for a traditional double-decker bus, in either long or shorter form.

Number 34 was originally restored by Carl Ireland in Hull. It then moved to the south east before coming north again to an enthusiast in Crewe. It was photographed above passing the boating lake as it came into Heaton Park for the Trans-Lancs Rally, and left, during the course of the event.

Number 91, seen opposite (and also overleaf) is part of the Boyle Street collection and is seen standing outside the Manchester Museum of Transport where that collection is housed. *(JAS all)*

The many special events organised by the Museum of Transport in Boyle Street, Manchester, provide opportunities to see preserved Stockport vehicles out on the road, and to ride on them. Number 91, above, is outside the entrance whilst 5871 in Selnec colours stands at Belle Vue, waiting to return to the Museum. Somewhat further afield, opposite, number 65 proceeds through the village of Exford, on Exmoor, where it operates a heritage service run by Quantock Motor Services. *(HP; JAS; CMC opposite)*

Senior Citizens trying to use their countrywide free bus pass to Chorlton on this service will be in for a very long ride! *(JAS)*

The Museum of Transport provided a vintage bus service in Heaton Park for some years, but difficulties with unruly elements in the Park led to this being curtailed and restricted to special event weekends only. Here number 97, converted to open-top configuration by the Museum, carries a good load on a glorious Sunday at the Trans-Lancs Rally which takes place every September. (JAS)